BIBLICAL STRATEGIES FOR WITNESS

BIBLICAL
STRATEGIES
FOR WITNESS

PETER MASTERS

THE WAKEMAN TRUST * LONDON

BIBLICAL STRATEGIES FOR WITNESS

© Peter Masters
This edition first published 1994

THE WAKEMAN TRUST
5 Templar Street
London SE5 9JB
ISBN 1 870855 18 3

Cover design by Andrew Sides

Printed in Great Britain by The Alden Press, Oxford

Contents

1. Inspiring and Maintaining Personal Witness

IT IS TAKEN FOR GRANTED throughout this book that readers are those who hear the words of the great commission ringing in their ears, and who want to see the Gospel of redeeming love spread throughout the district where God has set them. Perhaps it is not realised just how much detailed and practical guidance is stored in the Gospels and the *Book of Acts* for all who engage in personal witness and preaching. (Almost everything in this book is equally applicable to both personal witness and preaching, although the former is primarily in mind.)

Are we aware, for example, that the Lord Jesus Christ employed distinctive strategies for different kinds of unbeliever, and that these may be studied and copied? The Lord distinguished very clearly between people who were indifferent to their spiritual state, and those who were self-righteous, using quite different approaches to each group. It is not difficult to identify these distinctive methods of Gospel presentation in the preaching and witness of both Christ and His apostles. In addition, the Lord regularly employed several 'techniques' for opening the minds of all listeners.

Our Lord is not only a perfect Saviour and teacher, but a perfect example to us in all matters, and we must recognise and study the great wisdom of His methods. Do we know how to preach or witness to a particular type of unbeliever as Christ would have done?

Do we know how to stir the minds of both the heedless and the intellectuals, as Paul so wonderfully managed to do? Are we able to penetrate people's prejudices, sweep aside their suspicions, and secure their interest, as the Lord and His apostles did?

In this book every effort has been made to explore only the methods of the Lord and the apostles. We offer no wisdom or techniques of our own, not even the reasonable produce of human experience. There is more than enough to fascinate and stimulate us in the evangelistic example of the New Testament.

If readers want twentieth-century novelties and ideas, these pages will be of no help to them, for they are nothing more or less than an attempt to carefully observe the Saviour and His apostles, and to learn from them.

However, before proceeding with our examination of these unsurpassed methods, we must consider the biblical commands about personal witness, and various aspects of personal and spiritual preparation.

The ministry of personal witness is by any measure the most effective method for spreading the Gospel to multitudes of unsaved people. We certainly believe in the centrality of preaching, which has been especially ordained by God for the regular presentation of the way of salvation. But the Lord's chief method for bringing people under the sound of Gospel preaching has always been the personal witness of individual believers. Furthermore, personal witness is often the chief element used by the Holy Spirit in bringing a sinner to salvation.

In *Acts 8* we read of a great persecution against the church at Jerusalem, and of how Christians 'were all scattered abroad throughout the regions of Judea and Samaria, except the apostles.' Ordinary believers, few of whom were preachers, were driven out of their home city to take refuge in strange areas. But then we read of their reaction, and how they 'went every where preaching the word' (verse 4).

The Greek text says simply that they went everywhere *evangelising*. From the earliest days of the Church of Jesus Christ believers have obeyed the great commission in a personal way. Wherever they went, ordinary church members would be seen testifying to their faith and making known the Gospel. They firmly believed that the task of personal witness was ordained by Christ, their absolute Lord and Saviour.

Personal witness, however, is hard, and often risky. It makes us vulnerable to scorn and hostility. It may wreck a career. It may divide a family. It may cost us friends. It will often lead to embarrassment and repudiation. It is mostly a 'slow' ministry, involving, in the experience of some, months and even years of rebuff before someone responds. And for many Christians it conflicts with deep-seated natural shyness.

No wonder this duty slides out of view so easily. No wonder we prefer to focus our efforts on 'corporate' ministries, such as Sunday School teaching (though we would not for a moment minimise the importance of the Sunday School). No wonder we are inclined to leave evangelism to ministerial professionals. No wonder, in our churches, we would rather devise alternative ways, however elaborate and costly, of attracting in the 'unchurched'.

For this ministry we need constant encouragement and inspiration. These pages are an attempt to stimulate enlightened personal witness, though much of the material, as we have said, will hopefully be useful to preachers and speakers. A large part of the book looks at the strategies of the Saviour toward unconverted people. Other portions try to show the *real instrumentality* of those who witness and preach, for the sovereign God uses the biblical reasonings and persuasive arguments of His people in the regeneration and conversion of His elect.

We begin with a number of matters that need to be considered if personal witness (and, in the case of preachers, regular evangelistic preaching) is to be enthusiastically and effectively maintained.

1. A matter of conviction

To be kept up with quality, vigour and concern for souls, personal witness must be a matter of *conviction*. The personal witness texts must speak to our hearts with all their compelling and commissioning force. No congregation of the Lord's people will ever get down to serious witness unless the people are really convinced that God has commanded them to do this work. The hardest duties of the Christian life are only performed diligently and continually when we feel bound to do them by God's command. We cannot imagine a church without worship services, but, to the Lord's mind, a non-witnessing Christian is just as unthinkable.

Think of the words of the great commission: 'Go ye therefore, and teach all nations . . .' *(Matthew 28.19-20)*. Were these words of Christ spoken only to the disciples? Or were they spoken to them and also to their successors in all ages? Clearly to the latter, because Christ said, 'And, lo, I am with you alway, even unto the end of the world.' The commission is given to us all to reach out to everyone.

The well-known words of Peter show how the apostles taught the duty of witness: 'But sanctify the Lord God in your hearts: and be ready always to give an answer to every man that asketh you a reason of the hope that is in you with meekness and fear' *(1 Peter 3.15)*.

The Lord is to be given the highest place in our hearts, and witness is to be our central and supreme duty. Always we are to be ready to explain the Gospel and give our personal testimony, even if the question is asked by a persecutor (this being the context of Peter's words).

Paul, in *Colossians 4.5-6*, says much the same. 'Walk in wisdom toward them that are without, redeeming the time. Let your speech be alway with grace, seasoned with salt, that ye may know how ye ought to answer every man.'

In *Philippians 2.14-16* he tells us we are to shine as lights in the world, 'holding forth the word of life'. This exhortation is addressed not just to preachers, but to the ordinary church members of Philippi.

Do we obey the Lord in this? Do we have a testimony? Do we attempt to reach unconverted relatives, work-colleagues, fellow students, and neighbours? Are we constantly on the watch for opportunities in all our contacts? If not, do we feel no shame? Do we feel no compulsion to pray for help, and to improve? How will we ever face the Lord, if our lives have passed without our having obeyed Him and represented Him?

If we are firmly persuaded, as we ought to be, about the call and command of the Lord, then we shall be greatly spurred on in the work.

In recent years we have seen how a loss of conviction has destroyed the Sunday School work of many churches. It is an inescapable fact that the moment believers begin to lose their conviction about the necessity of evangelistic Sunday Schools, their vigour and interest wanes, and Schools close. Sunday School work is too arduous to survive unless there is real conviction in the hearts of the Lord's people.

The same is true of personal witness. It is only when we are convinced that God has committed to us the ministry of reconciliation *(2 Corinthians 5.18-20)* that we buckle down to witness. Only when we realise we have been commissioned by the Lord will we honour our calling.

Furthermore, we must bear in mind the great principle taught in *Ephesians 4.16*, which is that the growth of a church, both in soul-winning and maturation, depends on the full participation of *all* members. Paul speaks of – 'the whole body fitly joined together and compacted by that which every joint supplieth, according to the effectual working in the measure of every part, maketh increase of the body unto the edifying of itself in love.' If the individual members will not witness, the body will not grow.

We need to remind ourselves that on the Day of Pentecost the tongues 'like as of fire' rested on *each disciple*, because everyone was to be a light-bearer; a witness-bearer. Referring to *Ephesians 4.11-12*, we see Paul stating the ultimate aim of the preaching ministry, which is to perfect the saints for the work of all *their* ministry (this being the literal sense of the passage). Preachers have a responsibility to prepare, train and encourage the whole church family in the great task of witness-bearing.

We should not be surprised that in the *Book of Revelation* each local church is symbolised as a lampstand or light-bearer. Every believer is to be a living epistle – 'known and read of all men' *(2 Corinthians 3.2).*

What about God's anointing on great preachers? Is this not the way in which God, throughout history, has brought in the greatest spiritual harvests? Is it not through revivals and awakenings that the greatest blessings have come? How we would like the Lord to work in such a way that we would never have to toil! Sovereign grace revivals are indeed wonderful seasons of blessing. But where does Scripture say that the Lord will suspend the labour of human instruments during such times? The fact is that in revival God uses personal witness on a massive scale.

In the days when C. H. Spurgeon preached at the

Metropolitan Tabernacle, personal witness was far and away the principal means by which outsiders were introduced into the services. Even in revival years this was true. The membership records of the Metropolitan Tabernacle include a summary of the testimony of everyone who applied for membership during the entire Spurgeon ministry. These summaries show that the vast majority of converts were local, working-class people who were brought under the sound of preaching by the personal witness of Tabernacle members.

In the revival year of 1859, the overwhelming majority of those added to the Tabernacle's membership were first invited by a witnessing member at their work-place.

Not surprisingly, we find C. H. Spurgeon writing to his flock, while recovering from sickness, saying, 'I hope everyone will resolve to bring at least one stranger to hear the Word.' The people were used to hearing such exhortations, for it was the constant emphasis of the Tabernacle in those days. In prayer-meeting addresses Spurgeon gave such appeals regularly, and he paid frequent tribute to the 'great army of personal workers' within the church.

The best way of getting started in personal witness is to make this activity a matter of deep conviction. We must be biblically convinced that it is the God-given task of all believers to be continuously active in speaking of spiritual matters to those around them.

2. A matter of duty and conscience

We must not only seek to make personal witness a matter of conviction, but we must bind ourselves to perform it as a matter of *duty* and *conscience*. We know that a sense of duty adds further strength to conviction. If we have a conviction that the Bible commands us to witness, a strong sense of duty will add further commitment, determination and tenacity.

In *Romans 12* we are taught to present our bodies a living sacrifice, and this applies to witness as much as to other duties of the Christian life. There are times when a mother in the household feels too exhausted and jaded to get the dinner for the family. She is perfectly convinced, intellectually, that nourishment is necessary, but conviction alone will not always get the job done. At such times she acts out of duty and responsibility. When other emotions fail, duty motivates. We *must* do it! Here is the difference between conviction and duty.

It is our *duty* to get up and go to work. It is our *duty* to keep up our Christian service when the emotions are not co-operating as they should.

As far as witness is concerned, it is good to regularly ask ourselves, 'What have I done this week? What have I said for the Lord? Have I prayed for opportunities? Have I been a profitable servant or an unprofitable servant?' We must be troubled in our consciences if we leave off personal witness. Can we be comfortable as non-witnessers? Does our church allow us to feel at ease if we retire indefinitely from any personal effort at reaching the unsaved?

Special conscientiousness is vital for personal witness for the rather obvious reason that it is a form of Christian service for which there is no supervision. A vigorous church leadership may organise the Sunday School, the young people's work, the visitation and all the other 'corporate' ministries of a local church. But what about personal witness? What will happen when a believer is at business or college or caring for the home and family? The church leadership cannot help or stimulate in these places. The friendly pressure or rhythm of local church life cannot be represented there. The Christian is now alone and beyond the sway of organised service. It is in the lonely, unaided ministry of personal witness that a keen sense of duty and conscientiousness is most essential.

When Paul wrote to the Philippians he told them how much he valued their prayers for him, particularly that he would maintain a good witness during his impending trial and possible execution *(Philippians 1.19-20)*. Above all else he did not want to let the Lord down in the moment of testing. He coveted their prayers that he would be given boldness and Christian character. It was a matter of *conscience* with him that he should not fail the Lord.

Can we not teach ourselves and other believers to feel and to think like this? 'Woe is unto me,' says the apostle, 'if I preach not the gospel!'

3. A matter of desire

The ministry of personal witness must also be a matter of great *desire*. The apostle Paul tells us that he was prepared to endure all kinds of difficulties 'for the elect's sakes, that they may also obtain the salvation which is in Christ Jesus with eternal glory' *(2 Timothy 2.10)*. In his mind's eye he could see future believers – those who would be humbled and brought to love Christ – and for their sakes he would endure any difficulty to proclaim the Gospel to them. We too can remind ourselves that the Lord has a people in every place, and they are to be rescued, by the Gospel, from ignorance, folly, sin and pain. The Lord has posted us to our present situation in life to be a blessing to those who will be saved.

Then we must have great sympathy and feeling for all people. Think of Paul and his desire for the conversion of his countrymen. 'I have great heaviness,' he said, 'and continual sorrow in my heart.' He longed that they would see the Truth, and come to Christ. 'Brethren, my heart's desire and prayer to God for Israel is, that they might be saved' *(Romans 9.2 and 10.1)*.

To surmount the difficulties of personal witness we

need the driving force of pity and desire. We must *want* to be used by God. We must *long* to be a blessing to another soul. We must have a deep desire to please the Lord in this matter and to make a stand for Him. We must feel for people around us.

The Saviour sets us our example. He was so concerned about the people, that He lamented over the daughters of Jerusalem even as He went to Calvary. Whenever our feelings let us down, and we grow cold towards soul-winning, we must urgently pray that the Lord will invigorate us again and restore within us that essential concern for souls. We must fight against selfishness and self-concern, and have pity for the spiritual bankruptcy of others.

4. A matter of zeal

If our personal witness is to be anything more than a five-minute wonder, and if it is to cut through the apathy of those around us, then it must be characterised by *zeal*. King David said in *Psalm 69*, 'The zeal of thine house hath eaten me up.' When the disciples saw the great fervour of the Saviour, they knew that these words were the right standard for a true servant of God (*John 2.17*).

Epaphras laboured fervently in prayer for the Ephesians, because he had 'a great zeal' for them. Zeal is a Greek word meaning hot or boiling. It refers to great fervency. And this is what we should possess in the work of reaching lost souls. What is the difference between zeal and *conviction*, *duty*, and *desire*? Zeal is the practical energy of our being, with which these other attitudes must be clothed. It is the petrol for the car or the power for the lamp. It is the 'up-and-doing', and the vigour with which we perform. It is the opposite of languor or half-heartedness or mechanical compliance. It is so necessary to build up real fervour and zeal.

The epistles are full of stirring, martial language exhorting believers to *zeal*. We are in various texts commanded to be 'fervent in spirit; serving the Lord', 'striving together for the faith of the gospel'. 'Quit you like men,' says Paul, 'be strong!' 'It is good to be zealously affected always in a good thing.' Adds Jude, 'Earnestly contend for the faith.'*

The necessity of zeal must be emphasised today because the complexity and bustle of life exhausts and bemuses us to the point that we become relatively tame and insipid in our Christian service. Pastors everywhere find that today's society leaves Christian people worn out and intimidated.

Then there is another reason why zeal is so necessary. In the case of many Christians the work of personal witness is out of step with their personalities.

---

*Romans 12.11; Philippians 1.27; 1 Corinthians 16.13; Galatians 4.18; Jude 3.

They are shy and reserved, and making spiritual conversation proves difficult. For many others, their business circumstances give them surprisingly few natural opportunities.

We need to face up to the fact that witness is a matter of creating or setting up opportunities, and keeping up this work constantly. Witness requires a very definite effort against the general run of a shy personality, against our natural love of ease and a quiet life, and against difficult circumstances.

Often we know that we shall stir a hornet's nest. We know we shall create untold difficulties for ourselves. An application of initiative and energy, regardless of circumstances or consequences, is true Christian zeal. This may seem all very obvious, but we need to gird up our efforts constantly in this ministry. All must accept that here is a ministry which will never flourish without a considerable investment of committed effort.

Can we not be more like the apostle when he went to Athens? There his spirit was stirred within him because he felt so strongly his duty to witness to the idolaters of that place.

5. A matter of prayer

Personal witness is, of course, a matter of *prayer,* not only for vital blessings such as courage and ability, but also for *opportunities.* If we would only pray for opportunities we would surely be given them. The words of James must apply to witness as much as to other matters: 'Ye have not, because ye ask not.'

Even an apostle appealed for prayer that he would open his mouth boldly and speak as he ought to speak. He had found that his courage rose in answer to earnest prayer.

If we find ourselves working in a situation or place where there seems to be very little opportunity to draw alongside other people, then earnest prayer will sooner or later bring us face to face with someone who will listen. Perhaps we may even experience a dramatic change of circumstances or position, as the result of which our opportunities will increase.

Someone once said to this writer that after three days of praying for an opportunity he suddenly found himself confronted with an unexpected opening for which he was totally unprepared. His lack of faith in prayer led to his being completely caught out and tongue-tied. We need to pray very specifically for opportunities to arise, and to be ready for them.

6. A matter of forethought

The need to be ready leads naturally to the observation that effective witness is a matter of *forethought* and preparation. Some friends seem to think that witness, in order to be genuine, must be entirely spontaneous and unprepared. We have all heard of people who preach according to this policy. They imagine that a sermon, to be blessed of the Spirit, must be unpremeditated. Happily, most preachers recognise the folly of such a practice, and so should all believers engaged in personal witness.

Our great proof text for preparation is *1 Peter 3.15*: 'Be ready always to give an answer to every man that asketh you a reason of the hope that is in you.' (*Colossians 4.6* is another.) This ministry certainly requires pre-thinking. How do we intend to open discussion? How shall we answer the various questions which may come up? Do we have any plan, and do we have an *alternative* plan ready for those times when we are thrown off track by the common red herrings? Do we have any kind of strategy?

Later in these pages we make suggestions about the different approaches or 'tactics' which may be adopted, and we must never be ashamed to study witness in this way. We are engaged in a battle. We must know the prejudices which block people's minds from receiving the Truth of God and we must have very clear ideas about how we shall challenge them. (We shall comment further on the value of preparation in connection with promoting personal courage.)

7. A matter of skill and practice

We must be aware that personal witness improves greatly with the acquiring of *skill*. Forethought and preparation must rapidly become augmented by skill.

We must gain in craftsmanship as we rightly divide the Word of Truth (*2 Timothy 2.15*). Obviously we are not to become crafty, or to depend upon skill or techniques of argument. But we are to teach every man 'in all wisdom' and to 'walk in wisdom toward them that are without' (*Colossians 1.28* and *4.5*). The word translated *wisdom* has reference to practical skill or acumen. Skill can never win souls, but it enables us to present the facts of the Gospel simply, impressively (in the best sense of that word) and without fruitless digressions and detours being forced upon us by those to whom we witness.

Everywhere people follow hobbies which have become their passion. They read everything written on the subject, and bestow money and time to the limit of their ability. As Christians our all-absorbing passion should be to develop a worthy skill in witnessing for Christ.

The writer remembers hearing a group of veteran, inner city Sunday School teachers talking about their experiences with large and difficult groups of children. These teachers, both men and women, had truly learned the arts (and crafts) of getting on top of children. With them it was a matter of honour to know how to win and subdue a turbulent sea of youngsters. Each one had built up a memory store of anecdotes and approaches which would quell a riot and capture attention.

In the same way there is a 'craft' which can be learned for personal witness, and we should be learning and mastering such skills.

Every believer is *qualified* to witness for Christ. Every true Christian is commissioned and appointed by the Lord. But we all need to get on with the task and log some 'flying hours' if we are to acquire skills and fluency. With a little time on our side we shall handle our case with increasing ability; so the sooner we begin the better. Effective witness is definitely a matter of practice!

Above all, it is certainly a matter of the blessing of the Spirit of God, but as far as human instrumentality is concerned, practice (with thoughtful self-assessment and review) greatly improves witness.

8. A matter of courage

Witnessing is frequently a matter of *courage*. Even the apostle Paul, as we have noted already, though accustomed to all forms of hardship, expressed his need of courage, and asked for prayer that he might speak boldly. How can we increase our courage for personal witness? Surely by taking seriously the matters already mentioned. If personal witness is a matter of *conviction* and *duty* with us, and we therefore give ourselves no choice in the matter, this in itself helps to 'overrule' our timidity. Then, if we really do pray for a great *desire* to win souls, we shall be given a level of feeling which will act as a driving emotion, helping to silence the inner qualms of cowardice.

If it is a matter of *conscience* with us to witness, then this will aim a hammer-blow at our natural reticence. If, at the same time, we are driven by zeal to take *initiatives*, we shall be less inclined to shiver at the brink, nervously waiting for the perfect opportunity which will involve no embarrassment or difficulty.

And if we *pre-think our strategy*, much of our nervousness will be dispelled, because so much of it is associated with the uncertainty about how we shall fare.

It is worth noting that nervousness is often aggravated by us because we embark upon witness too suddenly. It is not necessary to launch into a nerve-racking encounter without any preparatory mention of spiritual things. Witness, ideally, should be introduced in a gradual way. It is rather like plunging into the cold sea. Some people rush straight in. Others cannot bring themselves to do that, so they do not go in at all. But there is a middle policy of gentle entry.

So it is with personal witness. We need not tax our nervousness to the limit and place ourselves under unnecessary pressure. We may successfully enter the act of witness one foot at a time, little by little, taking matters gradually.

We may offer people an item of Christian literature as an 'ice-breaker', so that they know where we stand

and may half expect some further discussion. It is comparatively easy to proceed in this way and it delivers the witnesser from all the tensions associated with hurling himself into the deep end of immediate testimony.

Equally we may talk about interesting events, experiences and people connected with our church, not necessarily as an introduction to *immediate* witness, but as a means of getting people accustomed to where our interests lie. Where circumstances allow, the gradual approach is a good antidote to nervousness. Above all, courage comes in answer to prayer.

9. A matter of patience

It must be said that witness requires great *patience* and stickability. Naturally speaking, every renewed burst of personal witness is likely to run down and fizzle out within a few weeks. We have to prepare ourselves to take up a *lifelong* ministry involving the patient pursuit of every opportunity.

Witness is also a matter of patience in the sense that we must not press people to yield to Christ instantly, by getting them to repeat an absurdly simple profession or prayer. Conversion is a deep work of the Holy Spirit, and we are not to 'make' or force conversions. Our task is to show people their need, to reveal God's remedy, to urge them to seek salvation, and to show them how. But we must always send them to Christ privately and personally, and then watch patiently. We are never to 'clinch' the matter, or put words into their mouths, or assure them that they are converted on the basis of an initial response.

Christian work is always a matter of continuous effort and great patience. 'In due season we shall reap, if we faint not.' From Moses to Paul, the Bible shows us how God's spokesmen have often waited long for their greatest seasons of ministry and usefulness.

Witness is bound to be hard, and patience particularly needed, because of the stubbornness and resistance of the human heart. We should also remember that much of our witness has a *negative* purpose. While we have the privilege of gathering in the elect of God and seeing souls won, it is also our task to prepare the ground for the day of judgement, that everyone may be warned and that God may be just when He judges those who would never turn to Him.

If we really believe that conversion is the work of the Holy Spirit we shall be prepared to wait for our presentation of the Gospel to be applied to the heart at any time during the hours and days following. When the rich young ruler turned away, the Lord did not detain him with a further cluster of arguments and expostulations.

We must allow the Truth to do its work in the heart of the hearer. We do not want to become complacent, or to neglect souls, but we must not intrude upon the

Holy Spirit's deep work in the heart. Patience is part of trust.

Patience is especially important when witnessing within one's family circle. Converted young people are apt to rush at the task of witnessing to unconverted parents. They cannot understand why their parents are so obstinate and so slow to grasp the Truth. Great patience is called for. We have heard many times of how acts of witness have led to family rows, all future witness being almost destroyed. In the family circle witness is unusually hard. It *must* be done, but not bull-at-a-gate style. Remember, time is on our side. Those parents may not seem to be listening, but they probably are, and they are *watching* also. The lives lived by their offspring will speak in the end and then, perhaps, the words will sink in.

10. A matter of simplicity

Personal witness must never be complex, jargon-ridden or conducted at too great length. The biblical example is to be seen in the discourses of the Lord Jesus Christ. His evangelistic messages were always both simple and graphic.

The capacity of unconverted people for understanding spiritual matters is very limited, yet our natural tendency is to say too much at any one time. If we really believe the truth of Paul's words that 'the natural man receiveth not the things of the Spirit of God: for they are foolishness unto him,' then we will not use too many arguments on any one occasion.

Of course, simplicity does not mean being childish. It means avoiding the use of elaborate and unnecessary intellectual arguments (which is often a cowardly way of avoiding a real act of witness). It means giving clear and unrushed statements of testimony, and giving uncluttered answers to spiritual questions. It means avoiding technical theological terms when there are everyday alternatives. It also means avoiding rushing from text to text as the Gospel is presented. Some friends tend to launch into witness like a certain style of preacher, quoting text after text at a breathless pace, and projecting an almost fanatical and brainwashed image. Simplicity is a good watchword for personal witness.

11. A matter of a definite aim

Personal witness involves having a very *definite* and *lofty aim* – that of being used by God to bring rebellious men and women to the place of true repentance. Such an aim will make it impossible for us to be satisfied with giving a few vaguely Christian sentiments. Some believers convince themselves that they are taking a great stand when all they do is make a little point now and then.

While we aim at conviction of sin and true repentance, we know that this is very difficult to achieve by personal witness alone. Ideally, witness must go hand in hand with preaching. Preaching, after all, has been designed by God to be more useful than any other form of communication for bringing souls under conviction of sin. It is certainly not the Lord's *exclusive* agency for this work, but it is His *chief* agency, according to the Bible. (The special significance of preaching is emphasised by Paul in *1 Corinthians 1.18-25.*)

Generally speaking we may find that our personal witness will consist mostly of spiritual testimony and basic Truth, coupled with invitations to services where there will be a closely personal Gospel challenge.

In our day, preaching is relatively powerless to attract a congregation. It depends upon personal witness to bring the unconverted hearers in. Personal witness, on the other hand, is often relatively powerless to bring souls under deep conviction of sin. God has made and moulded these two agencies to fit together in harmonious, soul-winning labour.

Therefore, in order to realise our ultimate aim of bringing people (by the work of the Spirit) to a *deep* sense of need and to conviction of sin, we need wherever possible to draw them under the sound of Gospel preaching.

12. A matter of spirituality and godliness

Last but not least, witness is a matter of *spirituality* and *behaviour*. *John 15* is but one of very many passages of Scripture which show that obedience to Christ is a condition of fruitfulness in this work. Our relationship with God must be right, and our conduct toward those around us must be sound. The ten commandments divide into these two parts, our duty to God, and our conduct in society. We need to ask ourselves: 'What sort of temperament do I have? Am I diligent in my work, or do I have a poor reputation? Am I a cold person? Do I come across as being somewhat vain or pompous? Am I peevish and impatient? How do I react in difficulties?

'Am I seen as a rather flippant person? Do I take seriously the duties of kindness and good works which are the essential foundations of effective witness? Do my reactions to trials show those around that I really do have contact with Almighty God, and access to divine resources?'

The self-righteous unbeliever who is diligent and conscientious in his or her job will despise the sloppy believer and disregard all he says. Some believers behave so poorly in everyday matters and in employment that one has to say that it would be better if they never witnessed!

The words of *1 Peter 2.11-12* provide an exhortation to witnessing Christians coupled with a promise: 'Dearly beloved, I beseech you as strangers and pilgrims, abstain from fleshly lusts, which war against the soul; having your conversation honest among the

Gentiles: that, whereas they speak against you as evil-doers, they may by your good works, which they shall behold, glorify God in the day of visitation.'

The godly life, the apostle assures us, will speak to unbelievers. The Holy Spirit will use it. Onlookers will be challenged, and some will be irresistibly drawn to Christ.

Is a godly life sufficient by itself? May I live a good life *instead* of witnessing? Peter leaves us in no doubt that the believers to whom he wrote *were* witnessing, stating that the pagans around them vilified them for their faith. The promise is that a godly life will come to the rescue of the word spoken, so that both will convince and melt those who are rebels against the Lord.

2. God Really Does Use Instruments

CLEARLY WE CANNOT go along with those who think that any unconverted person can be persuaded to receive the Gospel. We believe the Bible teaches that all people, by nature, are dead in sin, opposed to God and utterly unwilling to accept the challenge of God's Word. They will not repent of their sin or yield to the authority and government of God unless He, by His Holy Spirit, works in their hearts.

Conversion is a work of the Holy Spirit Who regenerates carnal hearts, illuminates darkened minds, and inclines rebellious wills so that sinners wake up to their spiritual condition, and come to repentance and faith.

If we go about the work of evangelism imagining

that the efficiency of our presentation will bring about conversions, then we massively underestimate the lost state of unconverted people.

However, we must not fall to the opposite error, which is that of feeling that there is absolutely nothing we can do to persuade sinners to receive the Gospel. There is a tendency for believers to go to either one extreme or the other.

Nowadays some teachers, in explaining the New Testament teaching on the new birth (or regeneration), go much too far. Missing the true sense of historic Calvinism, they say that regeneration by the Holy Spirit results instantly in conversion, so that the sinner suddenly discovers that he has faith in Christ, and is a Christian. In their desire to give all the credit for salvation to the Holy Spirit, these teachers reduce conversion to an entirely unconscious, 'passive' experience. They insist that when the Spirit regenerates a person, that person is immediately given all the spiritual faculties of a new-born believer, and consequently repents and trusts in Christ *as the result*, or the fruit.

The reader can see that this view removes the crisis experience from conversion. Seekers no longer pass through that moment or period during which they feel 'suspended' between being lost and being saved. They no longer repent as *unconverted sinners*, asking and longing for conversion. According to these teachers, if people truly desire to repent and trust in Christ, it is because they have been converted. There is no such thing as a seeker!

One well-known reformed preacher in the USA critically describes this view as 'zap' regeneration. All of a sudden you are converted, and the first step of faith is repentance. According to some who teach this view of regeneration, there is no point in trying to remonstrate with lost people, or persuade them to come to Christ for salvation. If they have not been regenerated, they will not understand what we are saying, and if they have been, they are already converted. What is the point of appeal, entreaty and persuasion (of the kind which Paul practised)?

One preacher who takes this 'totally passive' view of regeneration and conversion, tells us that all we can say to unconverted people is that they should listen to preaching in the hope that as the Truth washes over them, God will mysteriously regenerate them, so that they discover they have been converted!

We feel bound to warn that such a view of regeneration is far from authentic Calvinism, and is totally destructive to evangelistic witness. But sadly, many believers have been confused by these ideas.

Many preachers, influenced by this thinking, have lifted up their voices to say to their hearers, 'Repent and believe, and God will receive you, and transform you,' and they have been unable to finish the sentence. Half-way through, the thought has occurred to them,

'I cannot say this, because if any listeners feel inclined to repent and believe, it is proof that they are already converted.'

How can they preach the Gospel with persuasive, personal application if they hold this sad misunderstanding of God's regenerating act in a soul? And how can any believer witness effectively if held in bondage by this view?

The correct view is that of historic, mainstream Calvinism. This is the view so clearly expressed in the great confessions of faith of the 17th century. It affirms that God begins the work of conversion in a human soul by imparting life – regeneration. But while this is an instantaneous act, it results in (or issues in) the ongoing process of conversion.

Noted reformed theologian Professor Louis Berkhof is careful in his *Systematic Theology* to distinguish between two elements in regeneration, namely 'the beginning of the new life', and the 'bearing or bringing forth' of that life out of hidden depths. Dr William Hendriksen in his *Commentary on Romans* wrote of the 'initial stage' of regeneration which precedes conversion and faith. In other words, life must be implanted first (regeneration) before a person may be moved by the Gospel or understand its full implications. This implanted life will change everything, and the regenerated person will now certainly be persuaded by the Truth, and come to Christ.

Initial regeneration may bring about instant conversion the moment that the Gospel is first heard, or it may give rise to a period of seeking before the regenerated person 'finds'.

This is a mystery, as the Lord said it would be. 'The wind bloweth where it listeth, and thou hearest the sound thereof, but canst not tell whence it cometh, and whither it goeth: so is every one that is born of the Spirit' *(John 3.8).*

The essential point is that the sinner is not necessarily wholly and consciously converted by that initial act of regeneration. The process has begun. The outcome is certainly inevitable, because spiritual life is within. A new attitude to God, new sensitivity and understanding is now possessed. But, consciously speaking, the *immediate* result of regeneration is to produce a convictable, movable, desiring, earnest seeker.

The *Baptist Confession of Faith of 1689* describes the effects of regeneration very clearly. It describes how God effectually calls people by His Word and Spirit out of the state of sin and death which they are in by nature, saying –

'He enlightens their minds spiritually and savingly to understand the things of God. He takes away their heart of stone and gives to them a heart of flesh. He renews their wills, and by His almighty power, causes them to desire and pursue that which is good. He effectually draws them to Jesus Christ, yet in such a way that *they come absolutely freely, being made willing by His grace'** (italics ours).

Here we see how God's regenerating act affects minds and hearts so that sinners are drawn to Christ, but in such a way that they are made willing to come. In other words, as God plants the seed of life in a heart, that person immediately becomes open to the persuasions of the Gospel, and understands and willingly responds.

It may be that our words of witness, or our preaching, will be the means used by the Spirit, alongside regeneration, to bring a person to repentance and belief. God uses His servants; His messengers. And He uses the arguments of His Word to convince, convict, call and persuade the enlightened soul to yield to Him. Peter says we are 'born again, not of corruptible seed, but of incorruptible, by the word of God' *(1 Peter 1.23).*

Note how the *Baptist Confession* proceeds to elaborate on the point:–

'Man is dead in sins and trespasses until quickened

---

*This quotation is from the author's slightly modernised edition of the *Confession*, published by Wakeman Trust. The *Baptist Confession* uses exactly the words of the *Westminster Confession of Faith*. Anyone wishing to consult the Scripture texts on which these statements are based will find them listed in chapter 10 of either the *Baptist* or *Westminster* Confessions.

[made alive] and renewed by the Holy Spirit. By this he is enabled to answer the call, and to embrace the grace offered . . .'

The old-time Calvinists saw clearly that regeneration led to a 'process' of conversion (a process which could be extremely fast, or quite slow). People did not just wake up one day and discover that they had been converted, and that as a result they wanted to repent and believe. Regeneration launched them into a process of hearing the appeals of the Gospel with new ears, so that they were moved and convinced, and filled with longing to find Christ. It was worth urging them to repent and believe. Indeed, it was essential to do so, because this is the way God chooses to work in souls.

God means His children to go through the experience of being 'turned round' in heart and attitude. He means them to search and seek. He means them to be convinced by Gospel reasoning, and to consciously, personally, freely and willingly change their minds. To accomplish this, the Lord enlists us to go and witness and preach to people everywhere. Our message and our witness really counts in the glorious purpose of God. Without the Spirit, we can achieve nothing. But when the Spirit works, He uses our explanations, arguments and appeals.

This is why the Bible is crammed full of texts which say in so many different ways, 'Repent, believe, seek Me, and *I will* receive you, bless you, save you.' When a person is initially regenerated, it does not result in automatic and immediate awareness of salvation. It begins the conversion process, by which the sinner awakens, comes under conviction of sin, repents and believes, and yields to God. Then comes the *conscious* receiving of the full faculties of the new, converted life. Just as in human birth conception leads to the emergence of the baby after the period of gestation, so regeneration issues in a process which reaches its climax in *conscious* birth.

A great tide of texts throughout the Bible lays down the unassailable order – 'If you will repent and believe, then I, the Lord, will give you salvation.' Regeneration is certainly at the very beginning of everything. But there can be no doubt that sinners do not 'find' the Lord in a conscious way, nor receive all the faculties of the Christian life, until *after* they have called upon the name of the Lord.

We have considered this point at some length, but it is of very great importance. Our zeal for persuading lost souls of their need of salvation must not be undermined by a wrong view of the Spirit's work or the order of salvation. The Holy Spirit uses our words of witness. We realise that no one will turn to God unless the Spirit works, but we must speak as though people can understand. Persuasion is in the Bible. Among numerous texts affirming this, there is *Acts 18.13*, where the Jews brought this charge against Paul: 'This fellow *persuadeth* men to worship God.' And in *2 Corinthians 5.11* Paul tells us himself – 'Knowing therefore the terror of the Lord, we *persuade* men.'

This has been the conviction of all the great preachers in times of reformation and revival. This was the clear view of mightily used Calvinistic evangelists such as George Whitefield and C. H. Spurgeon. It was the firm understanding of the missionary pioneer William Carey and all who laboured with him. The list of those who pleaded with souls in a persuasive, wrestling, imploring presentation of the Gospel is *the* hall of fame of church history. To witness effectively, we must share their certainty about the importance and worthwhileness of witness.

3. Touching the Raw Nerve

HOW MUCH DOES the unbeliever understand about the existence of God? To what extent is he aware of his human sinfulness and need of forgiveness? Must we find a way of *intellectually* convincing our secular generation about the being of God, and of the everlasting validity of fixed moral standards? Is it necessary to begin every evangelistic sermon, or every witness encounter, with an attempt to prove by rational argument that God is there? Or can we assume that some awareness of God exists, and that people still have a conscience?

1. The directness of Paul's evangelism

One of the most helpful and encouraging passages in the Bible is the record of Paul's testimony before Felix and Drusilla recorded in *Acts 24*. Here we see clearly that when Paul preached or witnessed (even to those outside the Jewish tradition) he 'presupposed' that people already knew a great deal, or that they would intuitively recognise the truth of his teaching about God and salvation.

Felix was an utterly corrupt Roman procurator of Judea. Drusilla, his wife, was a Jewess (being a daughter of King Herod Agrippa I). Felix was steeped in Roman paganism. Along with his brother Pallas, he had originally been a slave, but both secured their freedom and rose to high positions in the state. Pallas became a chief minister and favourite of the Emperor Claudius, using his influence to get Felix appointed as procurator. The latter then built a terrible reputation for cruelty and avarice.

Drusilla was the second wife of Felix, having deserted her first husband (the King of Emesa) to marry him. Yet Paul spoke to this evil pair on the basis that they could easily understand their obligations to God.

Although Paul had previously given Felix a 'more perfect knowledge' of the difference between Jews and Christians, explaining that Christians literally believed the Scriptures to which the Jews merely paid lip-service, Felix was still a man of pagan understanding. In view of this we might well think that a series of lessons would be necessary to wean his mind from his religious and cultural background, enabling him to accept the Truth. We might well imagine, for example, that Paul would have to spend many hours proving that there was only one holy and just God, by contrast with the multiplicity of pagan gods.

We might wonder how Paul would set about explaining to Felix that so many things in his life were sinful. After all, sensual evil was paraded as a virtue in that society. It permeated all art and culture, and met with approval from leaders and gods alike. We might well feel that Paul would have special difficulty communicating the idea of a future day of judgement.

What, then, did Paul do with this abnormally proud and vicious man, so lost in the darkness of pagan ideas? Did he feel that it was more appropriate to establish the intellectual reasonableness of the Christian faith? Paul's example is very relevant to us today, in our godless and multiracial society.

The almost astonishing fact is that the apostle went straight to the point and spoke about Gospel matters. Consider the record of Luke in *Acts 24.24-25*:–

'And after certain days, when Felix came with his wife Drusilla, which was a Jewess, he sent for Paul, and heard him concerning the faith in Christ. And as he reasoned of righteousness, temperance, and judgment to come, Felix trembled, and answered, Go thy way for this time; when I have a convenient season, I will call for thee.'

The Greek verb translated 'reasoned' means – to 'lay

out' or thoroughly present the matter. What issues did he lay out before Felix? The issues of 'righteousness, temperance *[which means self-control]*, and judgment to come'. In other words he gave an extremely direct and challenging address. He proceeded on the assumption that as he described these things, Felix would have little difficulty in understanding them, and that his conscience could be touched.

This is not to say that Felix would necessarily be moved to deep shame, or show saving faith. These responses come only through the sovereign and irresistible work of the Holy Spirit. But at a human level, Paul could apparently count on the fact that there would be some answering chord in the heart of his hearer as he presented biblical truths. He was confident that Felix, at a mental level at least, would be able to grasp that these things were true, and that his conscience could be stirred.

Paul 'reasoned of righteousness' – or rather the lack of righteousness which renders people desperately in need of the mercy and forgiveness of God. Then he moved very specifically to self-control, putting his finger on the master sin of this notoriously violent ruler. Felix had always been in the grip of his sensual and impulsive heart. If he wanted anything, he *had* to get it, no matter who had to be eliminated in the process. So Paul focused on his most vulnerable and sensitive point, expecting to make an impact on the conscience. In addition Paul described the coming day of judgement when Felix, along with all others, would give account to God for all his sin. The apostle's message was unashamedly religious, and he certainly did not attempt an elaborate apologetic approach. Nor did he attempt to disprove Roman idols. He simply swept them aside. Luke emphasises this by recording that Felix listened to Paul – 'concerning the *faith in Christ*'. The apostle dealt with the sinner's desperate need of forgiveness and the converting power of Christ.

The effect, in the well-known words of the *Authorised Version*, was that 'Felix trembled'. Paul's direct and undiluted religious message did not bounce off this powerful and hard-hearted Roman, as one might have expected. Despite the governor's virtually amoral life, and the fact that he had been brought up under an entirely different religious system, Paul's assertions struck home with such penetrating power that he was seized with great fear.

Paul's *modus operandi* has enormous significance for us in an age when society has largely reverted to the paganism and immorality of the first century Greek and Roman world. In an environment where people no longer believe that sinful acts are sinful, or that God exists, we are inclined to think that we must *prove* that God is there, and that sin is sin. Paul, however, simply declared the truth about God, sin and judgement. He described the Gospel remedy, pressed the point, and pleaded with people to repent. He certainly did not emphasise the 'rational' or 'apologetic' approach, as though the pagan mind needed deliverance from a mountain of intellectual obstructions before people could understand or believe. He spoke as though the pagan mind could well understand what he was saying, regardless of whether they had ever heard such things before.

It is true that many people have already been judicially given up to uncleanness, or hardened by God because of sin, but we must assume some capacity to understand. (See *Romans 1.24* and *9.18*.)

From Paul's example we learn that our message has unique 'connecting' power, whether people show it or not. If we tried visiting our neighbourhoods and telling people about chemistry or atomic physics, the overwhelming majority of people would probably understand nothing. Our words would be incomprehensible to them. But when we declare the biblical message, every human being instinctively realises, to some extent, its truthfulness, and feels challenged. It may be that people will resist our message, hate it, and give no hint of being affected. But according to Scripture (as we shall see) they receive some challenge, and each one will be held responsible for his or her reaction.

As communicators, Christians are the most privileged people in the world. We are far more powerful than the industrialists who advertise soap powder on television. They cannot count on an answering chord deep in the soul of every viewer which says, 'Yes, I know in my heart that this message is true!'

Believers who think that every point of the Gospel must be rationally proved before it can have any effect are wrong. They impose upon themselves a huge extra burden of duty, not to mention much discouragement. At the other extreme, believers who think that worldlings can understand absolutely nothing at all without the regenerating work of the Spirit are equally wrong. These friends vastly underestimate the self-evident character of God's Truth, the self-accusing power of the human conscience, and the enlightened blameworthiness of the human race for its rebellion against God.

Of course, we hasten to affirm that a *deep and saving* response to the Gospel comes solely as the result of the regenerating work of the Spirit. But people are not complete blockheads. They are *people,* not *beasts,* and they are sufficiently capable of understanding our message to be held accountable by God on the day of judgement for their rejection of it.

2. *What do people know about God?*

Is Paul's directness of method confirmed by his teaching? Can we be absolutely sure that a straightforward Gospel approach will achieve a real impact upon the inner sensitivities of present-day, secular hearers? In *Romans 1* and *2* Paul shows how several aspects of our message will be plain and evident to all people, partly because they are made obvious by the natural world around them, and partly because they are indelibly impressed on each person's inner awareness.

Truths in this 'self-evident' category include the fact that there is one God, that He is invisible, powerful and holy, and that we are sinners destined for judgement. Although people may not consciously believe these things, once we explain them, they will carry a powerful ring of truth and considerable authority.

It is true that some parts of our message are not at all evident from nature, nor are they written in men's hearts. These parts include the way of salvation, the atoning death of Christ our Saviour, and how people may be forgiven, clothed with imputed righteousness, and born again. Such truths are revealed exclusively by the Gospel as Paul indicates in *Romans 1.16-17*: 'For I am not ashamed of the gospel of Christ: for it is the power of God unto salvation to every one that believeth; to the Jew first, and also to the Greek. For therein is the righteousness of God revealed.'

However, in all preaching and witness it is a great inspiration and encouragement to realise that the truths mentioned previously are even *naturally* receivable, no matter what class or culture our hearers belong to, and no matter how ignorant they may be, or how influenced by alien religious ideas. Consciousness of sin and guilt may be suppressed from conscious knowledge, but it is always there in the soul, lying just beneath the surface, so that the preacher or witnessing believer may stir it up.

Paul expresses this very plainly in *Romans 1.18-19*: 'For the wrath of God is revealed from heaven against all ungodliness and unrighteousness of men, who hold *[or rather, who hold down and so suppress]* the truth in unrighteousness; because that which may be known of God *[or about God]* is manifest in them; for God hath shewed it unto them.'

Many things 'may be known' about God even with the natural understanding, because these things are buried in our inner consciences and also shown to us by the natural world around us. Unregenerate people do not therefore have to be regarded as totally unreachable and unteachable, as though they were creatures from another planet. God has made them *inwardly aware* of His existence, and also surrounded them with the all-pervading evidence of nature, thus providing a double testimony.

Paul continues – 'For the invisible things of him *[God]* from the creation of the world are clearly seen, being understood by the things that are made, even his eternal power and Godhead; so that they *[all men]* are without excuse' *(Romans 1.20)*. Whether Paul is testifying to Felix, who venerated ancestors and emperors as gods, or whether in our own day we are testifying to secularists, the God we proclaim is obviously the only plausible, logical, true God. Even for those with unregenerate eyes certain things are plain, and may be clearly asserted with only modest sympathetic appeal to sense and reason.

Everyone may grasp, for example, that if there is a God Who sustains this world, then He must be *invisible* because no one possessing divine power is to be seen among the creatures occupying the visible world. The One Who possesses creating and sustaining power must be over and above us all, and invisible to us. This is so very apparent that the simplest mind or the smallest child can imagine an invisible God looking down upon His creatures.

Also, the very nature of creation tells us something about the character of God. Creation is so detailed and so marvellous. It breathes infinite wisdom, intelligence and design. It is obvious to people, therefore, that if there is a Creator God, He will possess amazing intelligence, vast knowledge, and boundless resources of power. Paul says that created things demonstrate 'his eternal power and Godhead' so very clearly that unbelievers are completely without excuse for their unbelief. They have no excuse if they choose to reduce their concept of God to something they can make with their own hands. The true God is the most natural and obvious concept to all people.

Equally it is perfectly easy and natural for people to grasp that this God will be a *personal* God, with a tender heart, because relational values are to be seen everywhere in the created world. Despite the cruelty and heartlessness of human beings we still see numerous instances of love, loyalty and kindness in human relationships.

The animal world reveals the same phenomenon. Everyone knows how even the lions look after their cubs with extraordinary tenderness. Among the most vicious examples of predatory nature there are numerous examples of affection and kindliness towards tiny and weak offspring.

It is therefore easy for people to accept that the God Who made our loving emotions and instincts knows all about tender love and compassion. Love and tenderness on earth must reflect something in the very heart of God. He must be a God of great feeling and kindness. Therefore, a message about a personal God Who is full of mercy and readiness to forgive is a message which every human being can grasp with comparative ease.

To take another aspect of God's character, everyone can see that the Creator is a God Who gives enormous attention to detail. This is all the more evident in the age of the microscope when we know so much about the astonishing beauty and complexity of things not visible to the naked eye. This all impresses upon the mind the capacity of God to mark each individual, to know all about each one, and to have a close interest in our obedience or disobedience.

Paul insists that the being and character of God are so obvious from the world around us, that we are all inwardly aware that there is an invisible, personal, everlasting, powerful Creator God, to Whom we owe praise, gratitude and obedience. But is it possible for people to miss these lessons of nature? Is it possible for these thoughts never to impress themselves upon the mind? No, replies Paul – 'They are without excuse. For even though they knew God, they did not honour Him as God, or give thanks' *(Romans 1.20-21, NASB)*.

The existence of one supreme God to Whom people are accountable is so apparent that if they fail to acknowledge Him, there is no possible defence or explanation which can be offered – this is the literal sense of Paul's words.

We see this reflected in the attitude of growing children to parents. As youngsters we all realise that we are our parents' children. We know full well that they work to provide for us, care for us and make all the necessary sacrifices for us, but because of our selfish hearts and rebellious ways we do not necessarily respect any of this, thank them or respond to them. We take everything for granted and frequently even resent our parents. It is not that we cease to believe that they exist or that they provided our home and upbringing. It is simply that we choose to shut out of our minds all sense of debt and accountability and behave as though we had a right to complete self-determination. That is an exact picture of how it is with God. We are instinctively aware that we are created by a powerful, invisible Being, but we choose not to give Him the credit, or to honour and serve Him.

3. How the conscience may be stirred

The result of human rejection of God is that He disappears from people's thoughts. Their awareness of Him slides out of consciousness. Paul describes this process when he speaks of how people were – 'vain in their imaginations, and their foolish heart was darkened. Professing themselves to be wise, they became fools' *(Romans 1.21-22)*. *Vain* means empty, and *imaginations* means thoughts.

The *foolish* and *darkened* heart becomes dull and depraved, so that the person lives as though there is no God at all. All awareness of God has apparently gone. But it has not entirely gone, for it is not far beneath the surface of the mind, and it can be readily stirred and resuscitated. To do this may produce a reaction of extreme annoyance, resentment and even hatred of God (and His messengers). But awareness *can* be stirred, by preaching and witness.

The unbeliever may not admit it but a raw nerve is touched when the Gospel is proclaimed to him. He may say with scornful defiance, 'How can you prove the existence of God?' He may chase down many diversionary alleys, but the Bible says that what may be known about God is obvious to him, and therefore his soul will be challenged. This is a wonderful incentive to the person who preaches or witnesses the Gospel.

But how can we be certain that this awareness of God can be stirred up again after many years of vain living? There are two strong and positive statements to this effect in *Romans 1*. The first is in verse 18 where Paul says that ungodly and unrighteous people – 'hold the truth in unrighteousness'. The word translated *hold* means here to hold down, or hinder or suppress the evidence of God. It implies that the unbeliever must apply constant pressure to keep the 'lid' firmly down, and so keep the evidence of God suppressed. We must remember that Paul is not just speaking of Jews, who were trained to believe in the one God, but he is also speaking of Greeks (with all their cultured idolatry) and barbarians (with all their superstitious darkness).

So the Word of God affirms that an awareness of God is always present in the heart, ready to be activated or perhaps inflamed. A second extremely powerful affirmation of this concludes and crowns the first chapter of *Romans*. Here the apostle goes even further by telling us that no matter how badly men may have fallen into sin and degradation, they *never* lose a suppressed awareness of their accountability to

God in a coming day of judgement, and this may be provoked into consciousness.

Paul first provides a long and terrible list of evil deeds, including heathen idolatry, homosexuality, atheism, fornication, vicious conduct and murder. Yet in spite of all, he tells us that an awareness of judgement is still alive as a basic instinct in people *(Romans 1.22-32)*. At the end of the list of evil deeds, he says about the evil-doers – 'Who knowing the judgment of God, that they which commit such things are worthy of death, not only do the same, but have pleasure in them that do them.'

The evil-doer sins against the 'pull' of an instinctual (if suppressed) awareness of his accountability to God, and is always capable of being challenged about his guilt.

The tense of Paul's words is important. Paul does not speak of sinners who *knew* the judgement of God, but of those who *currently* know about it. Every sinner is inwardly aware of God's decree – 'the soul that sinneth, it shall die.' People take pleasure in their sins even though they are aware (however dimly) that eternal punishment lies ahead of them.

The passage gives by way of example the sin of homosexuality. Even nature condemns this vileness, for people do things which they do not see even in the animal kingdom, and they should therefore be doubly aware of the disgusting and unnatural character of their actions. But Paul assures us that there is an even higher source of light convicting the homosexual, the light of conscience, for in common with all men he knows that there will be a judgement day for these things.

The homosexual may not choose to retain this fact in his conscious knowledge. He may suppress it out of sight *(Romans 1.28)*. But it is still there ready to be aroused by the messenger of Christ, and we may be sure that this sinner has a built-in fear of eternity; an apprehension of death, and a terror of the consequences of the grave, just like every other sinner.

In the case of some people, false teachers may have covered up this awareness with a blanket of error, training them to believe in some form of universal salvation. But it does not take much to rip the blanket off. Therefore, when we witness we will not have much reasoning to do, for as we explain and teach the true position it will activate an answering chord in the mind and heart of the hearer.

Whatever the darkness around us and however ignorant and far away people may seem to be, we may be certain that our hearers can follow when we go straight to the issues of sin and salvation. This will be true no matter how pagan our hearers may be, and regardless of their programming, background or prejudices, for ours is the clearest message in the world, and is completely self-authenticating.

Lest there should be any doubt remaining in our minds about whether unbelievers (for all their secular programming) have active consciences, Paul uses a compelling argument in *Romans 2.1* to prove the point. The fact that people possess a keen awareness of right and wrong is conclusively demonstrated by their readiness to judge other people by the true standards. Paul says – 'Therefore thou art inexcusable, O man, whosoever thou art that judgest: for wherein thou judgest another, thou condemnest thyself; for thou that judgest doest the same things.'

Everyone has the capacity to see evil in others. Everyone is ready to react when other people do things which are offensive, disgusting or wicked. Everyone is very quick to judge and condemn, proving that the true standards of morality and righteousness are present in every heart.

Furthermore, no one modifies or reduces their condemnation of others on the grounds that the offenders have been brought up under a different value system! This is because we all instinctively know that those other people also know in their hearts the true standards of behaviour, no matter what value system they have been trained by. Therefore there is no excuse for their bad or unjust behaviour. In our relationships with one another (especially between nations!) we make no allowances and accept no excuses. So, says Paul, by this censorious spirit unbelievers betray the fact that their consciences are alive and well, and leave themselves *inexcusable* in the sight of God.

4. *The instinctive knowledge of judgement*

Paul then goes much further and states that the unbeliever also has an awareness of the day of reckoning. He pictures unbelievers as people living life on two levels: 'Thinkest thou this, O man, that judgest them which do such things, and doest the same, that thou shalt escape the judgment of God?' *(Romans 2.3.)*

The key point of Paul's message here is that even the unbeliever possesses an inborn awareness of the reality of a coming day of judgement, so that his mind must actively engage in some reasoning or reckoning in order to allay all fear and concern, and so push the matter out of sight. Nevertheless, by this mental activity, the unbeliever shows that he knows within himself that there is to be a day of judgement.

In the light of this it is obvious that we need not be afraid of talking about judgement, on the basis that secular hearers could not possibly be expected to respect such a 'religious' theme. On the contrary, we should be encouraged to clear away the false assumptions which lead people to think they need not take this matter seriously. Most of them *will* inwardly respect our message, because deep down they know that they will one day be called to account for their lives. Our words, however gently put, may well meet with outward resentment and hostility, but this will only mark an inner attitude of subdued respect for what the soul recognises as the truth.

Paul proceeds to add yet another argument, showing that people may even have been conscious of the activity of God in their lives through some deliverance or survival which they have not deserved. He says (addressing unbelievers) – 'Or despisest thou the riches of his goodness and forbearance and long-suffering; not knowing that the goodness of God leadeth thee to repentance?' (Romans 2.4.) 'Do you despise?' means – 'Do you think lightly of, or under-estimate' God's kindness and patience towards you?

These words certainly applied to the Jews, for they had received great blessing and kindness from God as a nation, despite their notorious idolatry, but Paul is speaking to both Jews *and* gentiles, and he is speaking to them *as individuals*. His words therefore indicate that unbelievers may be aware (however vaguely) that God has been merciful towards them in not punishing grievous sins. The question is – have they drawn the right conclusions from their experiences, or have they thought no more about them?

Today, we may say to many unbelievers – 'Do you underestimate God's kindness to you in life? Have you not experienced moments when you have been in great fear, in deep distress or near to death, and you have come through these trials with a strange and humbling awareness that God has been merciful to you? Have you afterwards dismissed those thoughts? At the time you felt a sense of unworthiness for such a deliverance, and you felt that God had preserved you, but now the whole episode is an embarrassment and a nuisance to you.'

Whether Jews or gentiles, Paul shows that unregenerate people may have tasted something of the patience and mercy of God, but may have wilfully put out of their minds the notion that such experiences are designed to touch their hearts and to bring them to think again about their godless lives. They have refused to be affected. Nevertheless, many will remember how they once felt the tug of God's mercy upon their hearts, and as spokesmen for the Lord, we should be encouraged by this thought when we proclaim the message of salvation to them. Sinners are not always as insensitive as we may imagine them to be!

Paul nowhere tells us that unbelievers cannot understand what we are talking about. He does not say that they have not the remotest idea about God, or about His holiness, or about the day of judgement. He does not advise us to write scores of lengthy books on apologetics as the only way of introducing unbelievers to the faith.

Nowhere does he sanction the idea that we will have to prove every bit of our message inch by inch, step by step, as though unbelievers possessed radically different thought patterns, like aliens from outer space. On the contrary, he tells us that unbelievers are people who have a strong awareness of divine things within them, and who, because they are in conscious, wilful conflict with the Lord, are highly sensitive to challenge at various points.

5. God's judgement will assume that people knew what they were doing

Paul describes unbelievers as people who 'are contentious, and do not obey the truth' *(Romans 2.8)*. They will be punished with 'indignation and wrath' because their actions are carried out deliberately and in the light of clear awareness. This is the case whether the person is an 'enlightened' Jew or a totally pagan gentile *(Romans 2.9-11)*. Knowing that awareness and sensitivity are present, we are encouraged to step across the very threshold of their hearts to speak the gracious Gospel of our Redeemer.

The strongest possible confirmation of all these things is given by the apostle in *Romans 2.12-15*. Are gentile idolaters really capable of understanding so much of what we will say? Can people with no religious background be expected to understand about their sinfulness? Paul's words provide the answer:–

'For as many as have sinned without law *[as given through Moses]* shall also perish without law . . . For when the Gentiles, which have not the law, do by nature *[by instinct]* the things contained in the law, these, having not the law, are a law unto themselves *[ie: the law is shown to have been planted directly in them]*: which shew the work of the law written in their hearts, their conscience also bearing witness, and their thoughts the mean while accusing or else excusing one another.'

This passage speaks not of one, but of two 'faculties' within every person (even while unregenerate). Both of these carry the imprint of God's standards. God has written the standards of righteousness in the *heart*, and as if that were not enough, He has also created the independent faculty of *conscience* to bear witness to those standards. In other words, all human beings have moral standards indelibly stamped upon their instincts, *plus* a permanent, resident 'magistrate' (or better – 'counsel for the prosecution') accusing them of transgressions. So their inner thoughts are frequently thrown into conflict – the conscience accusing, and the rest of the mind excusing and justifying, their sin.

When we witness for Christ, we direct our words to minds and hearts which have been the scene of many an inner battle! Even where the conscience has been bludgeoned into inactivity, it has been sensitive in the past, and may be stirred up again. No human being ever completely forgets that he is a sinner in God's sight.

Final confirmation of this fact is given when Paul refers to the day of judgement as the day – 'when God shall judge the secrets of men' *(Romans 2.16). Secrets* here refer to things which are covered up or concealed. Every sinner has secrets. Every heart has a history of thoughts and deeds which are concealed from view.

No person on earth may know our most secret guilt, but *we* know it. The stench of guilt hangs particularly heavily on those things which we hide away, but one day all those secrets will be disclosed.

That vital word *secret* is a ringing reminder of the fact that *we know* what we are guilty of, even as unregenerate people. We do not merely have *sins*, we have *secrets*, for we know what we have done, and the fear of shame forces us to hide it from view.

6. The apostles held people responsible

What an insight all this gives us into apostolic preaching. How much it helps us to understand what the apostles were doing when they preached. When they preached of judgement, their word had the effect of stirring up those secrets and causing people to remember them. So the hearers were given a view and a reminder of the state of their own hearts.

When the apostles preached, they would survey the people and say to themselves: 'Half my Gospel you potentially already know, and I will stir up your instinctive knowledge and compel your heart to acknowledge the Truth. I am going to draw attention to the things you have done, help you to see your great spiritual need, and then describe to you what the Saviour has done for sinners who come to Him.'

This was the stance of the apostles. They knew that their message was self-authenticating and powerful to a considerable extent *even in the absence of true, saving faith*. And this was the attitude which they passed on to the next generation of preachers. Note the confident triumphalism and authority in the words written by Paul to Timothy –

'I charge thee therefore before God, and the Lord Jesus Christ, who shall judge the quick and the dead at his appearing and his kingdom; preach the word; be instant in season, out of season; reprove, rebuke, exhort with all longsuffering and doctrine' *(2 Timothy 4.1-2)*.

While these words are certainly not to be taken as a licence for a bullying, hectoring style of preaching, they show the Gospel messenger as a person who addresses wilful and responsible rebels who have enough light and awareness to be called to account by the Judge of all the earth. These are the people whom we teach, and with whom we remonstrate and plead. And we must do this inspired by the realisation that needy sinners understand so very much of what we say, whether they show it or not.

Sometimes we underestimate the extent to which

people are aware of divine things by overstating such texts as *1 Corinthians 2.14* – 'But the natural man receiveth not the things of the Spirit of God: for they are foolishness unto him: neither can he know them, because they are spiritually discerned.'

It is perfectly clear that saving illumination is essential if people are to come under genuine conviction of sin, see their spiritual need in all its true depth, and feelingfully grasp the message of the atonement. There is no argument about that. But even without this vital illumination people's minds are aware of a number of fundamental spiritual matters, and biblical evangelism must be based upon this fact.

If we fail to appreciate these matters, then we shall think of people as virtual blocks of stone or as amoral beasts, unable to know anything about God without a massive campaign of apologetic reasoning. We shall take the view that people are too far away for any direct conversation on the fundamentals of the Gospel, and will first attempt to convince them about the existence of God, and about the existence of sin and guilt. We will worry about our message having intellectual respectability. We will concentrate on 'evidence' for the faith, and talk about the 'reasonableness' of our faith.

By underestimating the capacity of people to understand anything, we become semi-rationalists. We end up treating people as though we do not believe that they were made in the image of God in any meaningful sense, or that they are responsible for their sin!

Some believers (as we have observed) go even further in their underestimation of how much people can understand. They take the view that, unless the Spirit moves, people are in total outer darkness as far as divine things are concerned, and conclude that there is no point in broaching spiritual matters at all. Unconverted people must be persuaded to read the Bible or place themselves under the sound of preaching, in the hope that the Lord may suddenly regenerate them to life and enable them to understand. Without God's intervention, there is no hope of their grasping *anything* that we say. Such views obviously quench persuasive witness and make evangelistic reasoning irrelevant.

Once again it is affirmed that the regenerating, quickening work of the Spirit is essential to a *saving* understanding of spiritual things. But even without this, all people have a degree of awareness which we have the privilege and duty of stirring up, and they have a capacity to understand the fundamentals of our message at a mental level.

The quickening of the Spirit awakens mental powers and causes people to reason correctly in the light of what they hear. He gives them a desire and willingness to respond to the Truth and to yield to Christ, which would otherwise seem entirely unattractive to them.

He enables them, by His regenerating power, to desire heavenly blessings and to see through the pleasures of sin. All this is absolutely vital to salvation, but even without it, men and women have a measure of understanding and feeling, and must be challenged by the Word. They are still responsible to God, and God will one day judge them in accordance with what they have heard. Furthermore, should the Holy Spirit illuminate their minds and incline their hearts, He will still use the arguments and remonstrations of those who preach and witness the Gospel. By these very means the Holy Spirit will speak to their hearts, drawing them to personal faith in Christ.

7. Is any apologetic material useful?

What, then, about the place of apologetics in all this? Is it necessary to convince people's minds, at very great length, about each element of the Truth? The answer is that it is not necessary. Certainly, a modest measure of apologetic material may be extremely helpful for various reasons. While it is unnecessary to *prove* the faith to people, yet an apologetic element in our presentation may add considerable interest and serve a similar function to that of the parables and other illustrations used by the Lord.

A proportion of apologetic material may also help to assure our hearers that we are not 'flat earth' obscurantists! We shall show sympathy and appear willing to help them come to terms with some of their vaunted intellectual stumbling-blocks. But really, we know that their problems are rooted in the heart.

In the modest use of apologetic material we are seen to be sympathetic to the condition we find them in, and this is surely a worthy stance for those who represent a loving Saviour. Therefore, while apologetic reasoning is unnecessary, we may see it as a purely secondary or supplementary means of catching interest and making our communication attractive, and dealing sympathetically with the various intellectual 'hang-ups' unconverted people may have.

We should derive tremendous encouragement and inspiration from the fact that unconverted people have a raw nerve which may be touched, and an instinctive awareness of the God to Whom they are accountable. This should greatly inspire us and guide our words in all our preaching and witness.

4. Strategies for Different Kinds of Unbeliever

THE LORD JESUS CHRIST and His apostles have provided a perfect example of searching, challenging witness targeted to the disposition of hearers. As we trace the Lord's discourses and encounters, we see that certain strategies or approaches occur repeatedly. We need to note the methods of our Saviour, recognise their divine genius, and then employ them. The most striking aspect of these examples is the way in which the Lord dealt with different *kinds* of unbeliever in different ways.

If readers are familiar with the classic work of Charles Bridges, *The Christian Ministry*,* they will

---

*First published in 1849, and now published by The Banner of Truth Trust.

recall that this point is convincingly made in the final chapter of the book. Bridges provides a summary of the pastoral treatment of several different classes of unbeliever, together with some selected Scripture passages showing how the Lord dealt appropriately with each one. He lists six classes of unbeliever.

1. *The infidel,* by which he means the person impatient of all moral restraint and scornful of God. Today, we would use the term *atheist.* Bridges speaks of the *sensual* infidel (who is all lust), the *imitative* infidel (most often a younger person who naively accepts atheism with little thought, and then retails its arguments), and the *shrewd* infidel (or the militant, intellectual atheist).

2. *The ignorant and the careless person,* who does not think about the soul and does not seem to worry. He may nominally accept the religious teaching of his upbringing, but it makes no impression on him.

3. *The self-righteous person,* who is entrenched in a system of external religion, without faith, love, repentance, separation from the world, spiritual desires, or dependence on the mercy of God.

4. *The false professor,* who has intellectually accepted the faith and joins in worship, but has no personal experience of conversion.

5. The person who experiences *natural and spiritual convictions,* even to trembling and fear, and yet

cannot be induced to seek after salvation.

6. *The backslider*, who is, of course, not strictly an unbeliever, but who may be living as such and in a very hardened condition.

Charles Bridges points out that Gregory the Great listed thirty-six categories or dispositions of soul (though with 'scant exercise of spiritual discrimination'). Martin Bucer, who wrote extensively on the pastoral case categories in the 1540s, is praised by Bridges for his 'accurate and instructive distinctness'.

Other preachers of the past, especially of the Puritan period, have also recognised and classified different classes of spiritual condition, particularly among unbelievers.

It is this time-honoured theme which we now pursue, seeking to discern the variation of approach taken to each 'unbeliever-category' by the Lord and His disciples. We shall confine ourselves to a study of the four chief categories:–

1. Ignorant and indifferent people.
2. Self-righteous people.
3. Self-interested people.
4. Convinced atheists.

The Lord constantly pointed to different kinds of unbeliever in His parables as He described people to themselves. The parable of the two sons *(Matthew 21)* distinguishes between the self-righteous and the repentant rebel. The parables of the wedding feast and the great supper *(Matthew 22* and *Luke 14)* identify the ignorant and indifferent, the self-interested, the militant haters of God, the self-righteous, and the unworthy recipients of grace.

The parables of the talents and the ten pounds *(Matthew 25* and *Luke 19)* identify atheists, the self-interested, and the obedient. The parable of the two debtors *(Luke 7)* contrasts the self-righteous and the repentant. The parable of the prodigal son and the elder son *(Luke 15)* compares the repentant atheist with the unrepentant self-righteous person.

The parable of the sower *(Luke 8)* includes several spiritual states, represented by the wayside hearer, the rocky ground hearer, the thorn-patch hearer and the good ground hearer. In this parable, as in others, people are invited to see themselves, and consider their standing before the Lord.

The wayside hearer is the person who lives on the highway of worldly desires, events, fashions and pleasures. His mind and heart are hard, and the seed bounces off the surface of his understanding. He is firmly closed to the Gospel, representing the indifferent person, and perhaps also the atheist.

The rocky ground and thorn-patch hearers have real interest, but it does not last. They clearly represent the self-interested class of unbeliever (as we note in a later chapter). Their worldly interests eventually prevail in their lives. The good ground hearer is the person whose heart is prepared and humbled by the regenerating work of the Spirit to receive the message of redeeming love, and to repent and yield wholly to Christ.

A word of warning must be sounded here. Parables such as these, distinguishing between states of unbelief, must not be read or expounded in a fatalistic way. Some people fall into this trap. They say, for example, that the wayside hearer is a hopeless case. He represents a heart untouched by the Spirit, and can never therefore hear, understand or respond and be saved. But the purpose of the Saviour is not to distinguish between those who will and those who will not be saved. It is to warn people that if they fit into a 'bad' category, they cannot be saved *while in that state.*

Perhaps, even as the Lord described these 'bad' categories, the Spirit illuminated the hearts of people and awakened them to see their state, so that by a mighty work of convicting grace they were transferred into the better category of 'good ground'.

As we describe these different spiritual states to people (whether in witness or in preaching), we long that God will cause them to see themselves, and repent. We are to witness and preach, not to crush or condemn, but to stir, provoke, invite and implore people to come to a better attitude, namely, that of belief and seeking after the Lord. We trust in the mighty power of God to use our words to jolt and to draw needy souls. This is the only fitting approach to Gospel work, and in this spirit we study the four main categories of unbeliever.

5. The Ignorant and Indifferent Person

W E BEGIN WITH the largest class of unbeliever, that of ignorant and indifferent people. What approach may we take to those who seem totally unconcerned about their souls? How can we find a way to stir, trouble or interest their minds?

Such people are completely earth-centred in their outlook, hopes and aspirations. Their minds are saturated with matters of home and family, work and colleagues, pleasures and pursuits such as films, videos and TV programmes. Some know everything there is to know about the stars of stage and screen. By contrast, their consciousness of spiritual and eternal matters is zero. Any knowledge they may have about the faith is far too vague to be of any use to the soul.

Unfortunately the ignorance and indifference of this category of unbeliever is reinforced by what they see of the religious scene. All they observe is an unattractive world of waffling clergy, robes, candles, muddle and decline. It is a scene of weakness and irrelevance, and of religious leaders at loggerheads over various issues such as the ordination of women.

The unbeliever's general impression of Christians (viewed through the state church) is that they are a bunch of strange do-gooders with very naive ideas about human affairs. Worst of all, they do not know what they believe, except that most no longer think that events such as the resurrection really happened, or that hell actually exists.

1. The strategy of dissociation

In trying to witness to ignorant and indifferent unbelievers whose minds have been poisoned against Christianity, where shall we begin? Did the Saviour face similar difficulties? Did He have a specific approach for them? The answer, of course, is that He did. The great majority of ordinary people among the Jews of Palestine in our Lord's time were ignorant of the true message of the Bible (salvation by faith alone), and also completely indifferent. Indeed, they were more indifferent than the gentiles, because they thought that all Jews automatically enjoyed good standing with God, and this led to staggering complacency. As far as the masses were concerned, their disinterest in spiritual matters was buttressed and excused by the blatant hypocrisy of their clergy – the scribes and Pharisees.

What, then, did the Lord do to arouse their interest and concern, and make them listen? We observe that, *always*, the first step taken by Christ was to drive a wedge between their mistaken ideas about religion, and true faith. He did this by repudiating the formal, nominal, powerless religion of the day, and discrediting its teachers. As He did so, crowds would be astonished and would crane forward to listen to what He taught in its place.

The Saviour always went about this in a most dramatic way. He would often wait until a tremendous crowd had gathered, and the scribes and Pharisees were close to hand. Then, in the hearing of all the people, He would expose their hypocrisy and error.

Once, when one of the greatest crowds of all gathered *(Luke 12.1)*, the Lord opened with the provocative statement, 'Beware ye of the leaven of the Pharisees, which is hypocrisy.'

Some of those religious leaders came under conviction (such as those mentioned in *John 12.42*), though most became further inflamed in their hatred for Him. But the great crowds woke up to the fact that the Lord brought them something totally different from the cold, formal, ritualistic religion of the scribes and

Pharisees. In other words, the Lord employed the *strategy of dissociation* to jolt the minds of the people. He distanced Himself from false religion in order to create interest in the distinctive message which He brought.

Like our Lord, the first thing we have to do is to distinguish between genuine Christianity and the perversion or distortion which most people today hold in contempt.

In Britain most unbelievers get their first view of nominal Christianity from school assembly and classroom, and this usually consists of woolly, weak, theologically liberal ideas. As life goes on, they attend the occasional wedding or funeral, or see non-evangelical clergy speaking on the television. Naturally they are unimpressed by the effete, insincere and generally irreverent image they so frequently project. It is vital that we dissociate from such dead, formal religion in order to surprise people and open up their minds to what is true. Dissociation never fails to surprise people. To point out that the nominal clergy teach the opposite of what traditional Christians believe is bound to cause surprise.

In tracing the Saviour's approach to large crowds of generally indifferent people, we note that dissociation from error is the first and major strategy, and was effected as a shock tactic to produce the greatest measure of surprise. In due course we shall add another element – the use of strong pictures or illustrations. Readers are invited to observe in their study of the Gospels that these elements are *always* used by Christ when addressing the ignorant and indifferent masses.

In the Sermon on the Mount we have one of many examples of the Lord addressing a great crowd of people normally indifferent to spiritual things. Yet He spoke in such a way that they were – 'astonished at his doctrine' *(Matthew 7.28)*.

As ever, the Lord made use of shock tactics, or the element of surprise, using stunning words to dissociate Himself from the religious *status quo*. The sermon opened with the Beatitudes – sentences full of the unexpected. Here was a description of people vastly superior to the religious leaders in spirituality, humility and sincerity. And soon enough the Lord made a statement so surprising that it sent shock waves of amazement and even bewilderment through the crowds. Consider the impact of these words: 'For I say unto you, That except your righteousness shall exceed the righteousness of the scribes and Pharisees, ye shall in no case enter into the kingdom of heaven' *(Matthew 5.20)*.

This was a devastating blow to the prevailing teachers, but thousands of people who had long been unimpressed by the sanctimonious humbug of their religious leaders began to take notice.

What does it do for unbelievers in our society when they see the televised Remembrance Day programme at the Royal Albert Hall, and observe the chief clergy reading Scripture in strange, pompous, insincere tones, and 'praying' with their eyes wide open? Such travesties of true religion only seal people in their derisive rejection of the Christian faith.

We must imitate the Lord in dissociating ourselves from such nonsense, and tell people that unless a man's Christianity is more *alive* and *spiritual* than that of popes, archbishops, and so on, he will never go to Heaven. Did not the Lord tell the people that most of their professional clergy would never go to Heaven because their religion was not authentic?

Throughout the Sermon on the Mount the scribes and the Pharisees remained an essential 'visual aid', and no act of dissociation could have been more public or more emphatic than the exhortation: 'Take heed that ye do not your alms before men, to be seen of them . . . Therefore when thou doest thine alms, do not sound a trumpet before thee, as the hypocrites do in the synagogues and in the streets, that they may have glory of men. Verily I say unto you, They have their reward' *(Matthew 6.1-2)*.

This was the kind of comment those arrogant religious leaders were forced to listen to in the presence of great crowds. Repeatedly the Lord placed a great gulf between Himself and the false teachers, calling them hypocrites, and charging them with seeking the admiration of men. Numerous scriptures relate this use of surprise and dissociation in our Saviour's ministry. It was essential to begin at this point. The spiritually ignorant and indifferent masses had to realise that His teaching had nothing in common with what they had always imagined was 'standard' religion.

The position is the same today. People imagine that they know what the Christian faith teaches. But what they scorn is only a tragic perversion of it. We long to see people register surprise as we repudiate this, and hear them say, 'Well, what *is* right? What do *you* teach?'

2. Opening the mind: arousing intrigue

The entire method of Christ from the very beginning of the Sermon on the Mount is highly intriguing. The record tells us that 'when he was set, his disciples came unto him: and he . . . taught *them,* saying . . .' *(Matthew 5.1-2).*

Now this provided a remarkable visual lesson in itself, and a great surprise for the watching crowds. The Jews were convinced that they were God's chosen people by virtue of their race, and yet here was something novel and jarring. Christ gathered His small band of special followers around Him, and in full view of the crowds began to address *only those disciples,* as though they alone were God's children. He did not immediately state that the rest of the listening crowd were outsiders and only His personal followers members of the kingdom, but his *visual* method conveyed this.

He said only the humble would have the kingdom of Heaven, and only those who hungered and thirsted for righteousness would be satisfied. He said only the genuine and sincere would ever see God. He said such people would be persecuted, and told them they were the salt of the earth and the light of the world.

How astonished the crowds must have been to hear Christ indicating that the Jews in general were not in God's kingdom, but only the disciples – His personal followers! In their state of surprise, the crowds listened as they had never listened to anyone before. Then, as the sermon proceeded, the Lord corrected the false teaching of their tradition about, for example, divorce and revenge *(Matthew 5.31-32 and 38-40)*.

Later in this wonderful sermon the Lord again distanced Himself from the religious leaders, condemning their hypocrisy and showmanship *(Matthew 6.1-5)*. Then He created a hearing for positive evangelistic teaching. He spoke about genuine prayer, and He also showed the people the tremendous difference between the life which is lived for the here-and-now, and the life which is lived for God (eg: *Matthew 6.19* – 'Lay not up for yourselves treasures upon earth,' etc). He urged them – 'Seek ye first the kingdom of God, and his righteousness' *(Matthew 6.33)*.

Using graphic language (a practice we shall comment on shortly) He built on the foundation that the people should not presume themselves to be God's children, by showing that God must be personally sought and found. 'Ask, and it shall be given you; seek, and ye shall find; knock, and it shall be opened unto you' (*Matthew 7.7*). Personal faith, and the seeking-finding concept, is as surprising today as it was then.

The miniature parable of the two gates and the broad and narrow ways divided humanity (including the Jewish listeners) into those on a road to everlasting life, and those (the great majority) on a road to destruction (verses 13-14). The Lord did not start by condemning their sin, but He intrigued them with the 'insiders' and 'outsiders' concept.

The Lord's Jewish hearers must have been shaken out of their complacency and presumption by the words, 'Not every one that saith unto me, Lord, Lord, shall enter into the kingdom of heaven; but he that doeth the will of my Father which is in heaven' (verse 21). Then He gave the parable of the houses built on rock and on sand (verses 24-27), distinguishing between the person whose life is mere outward show, and he whose everlasting soul is secure.

Constantly, here, we see in the Lord's presentation, material to surprise, stir interest, and open the mind. The long-standing opinions of the people were challenged, and their notions of religion confounded.

Though warm and compassionate in tone, the Lord's words challenged their standing, and pointed to a special experience of God.

3. Stressing the eternal context of life

A special aspect of the Lord's approach to the ignorant and indifferent was His stress on the eternal context of life. This was supremely manifested one day – 'when there were gathered together an innumerable multitude of people, insomuch that they trode one upon another' *(Luke 12.1).* On this occasion the Lord gave that captivating parable of the rich fool, aimed at jolting the people into realising the empty vanity of a life lived solely for material things.

The entire passage demonstrates the Saviour's use of an unusual and richly graphic illustration to stir the minds of His hearers. People in their thousands were prised out of their lethargy and indifference as they listened, and their prejudice and complacency were temporarily thrown aside.

When confronted by that conspicuously vast multitude the Lord employed *dissociation* as His first point (verses 1-2) and proceeded to talk about the eternal soul for His second (verses 4-5). For His third, He touched upon the fact that Almighty God knew all about them from the hairs of their head to every word they uttered. The parable of the rich fool – a message on spiritual foolishness – laid the axe to the root of spiritual indifference. Repeatedly in this discourse the Lord stressed the eternal context in which life is lived, each illustration and point falling as a hammer-blow on the hard shell of human complacency. The solemn words – 'And if he shall come in the second watch, or come in the third watch . . .' – warned of the uncertainty of life, and the approaching moment of account (*Luke 12.38*).

4. Using illustrations

A most significant lesson in the Lord's method is given in *Luke 15*. An extraordinary crowd of tax gatherers and notorious sinners gathered to listen one memorable day when three famous parables of grace were uttered – the lost sheep, the lost coin and the lost son. In these, true spirituality was portrayed as returning to God; a matter of being found and possessed by Him. Imagine the effect as wealthy and self-confident people saw themselves described as lost, disadvantaged, purposeless, wasting away and doomed!

Yet even in this discourse the Saviour took time to distinguish between His teaching and that of the religious establishment, though in the most tender way. He exposed the proud resentment of the elder son, who would have nothing to do with his father's amazing grace, and it was obvious to all that the Pharisees were depicted.

In the discourse about the rich man and Lazarus

(Luke 16.19-31), the Saviour wove His teaching on Heaven and hell into a picture which held the crowd spellbound. Here also was the element of surprise, because Jesus taught that the religious leaders, who were imagined to be so privileged and blessed, faced humiliation and eternal misery.

Such illustrations as the good and the corrupt tree emphasised the need for a radical personal change; a conversion. Any attempt to be 'religious', other than by obeying Christ and receiving a new life, would lead to failure and disaster.

5. Applying the Lord's methods today

Like the Lord, we must attempt to capture the attention of ignorant and indifferent unbelievers with surprising statements and interesting illustrations. We must show that true religion is nothing like the travesty and caricature which they have in their minds. It will only be as their false assumptions are swept away that their minds will be opened to listen to words which explain Christianity in terms of a great change, a new life, and a definitely felt, personal, spiritual relationship with God, leading to Heaven.

How can we surprise people today? Here are just a few fairly familiar examples of points which we can profitably make in our regular 'forays' into the strongholds of indifferent unbelievers.

For example – it generally comes as a great surprise

and shock to the ignorant and indifferent person to discover that Christianity was never meant to make the world a better place. The unbeliever, when he thinks of religion at all, is bound to view it through very earthly eyes (as did the Jews of old). He assumes that it is offering something which will benefit people in the way *they* want to be helped. To be of any value, religion must be able to make their lives happier and more prosperous.

It comes as a surprise to people to be told that the Christian Gospel has no plans to improve earthly society and make rebellious people happier. God has no intention of blessing and improving a world in a state of hostility to Him, its Creator.

Very often, the reaction of an unbeliever on hearing this is to think, 'Then what is God's purpose?' At this point the truth can be stated about the *spiritual* plight of man, and the *spiritual* mission of God to save souls eternally. We can speak of God's remedy for man's rebellion, and the nature and result of genuine conversion to Christ.

Then again, it always comes as a surprise to worldly people to discover that (as one preacher used to say in the early part of this century) 'Christ was the greatest pessimist ever about the fortunes and future of this world.' It surprises people greatly to learn that the Lord had only a message of doom about the progress of mankind. The indifferent person usually imagines that Christianity is smilingly *optimistic* about the future of the world and society. When we tell such people that Christ predicted wars and rumours of wars up to the very last day, a puzzled frown appears, and they often begin to listen.

Further, it frequently astonishes the non-churchgoer to hear that true Christians do not believe that man is good at heart. For some reason (perhaps from being wrongly taught in school) people assume that Christians are optimistic about human nature. It rather shocks them to discover that we regard *them* as being naive about human nature, and that *we* have the gloomiest possible view about the human heart and character.

All these points can be so made that the element of surprise will help to open up the mind of the listener. Then we can explain depravity, the Fall, and man's alienation from God.

The total outsider is very likely to imagine that the Christian faith teaches that good people will get to Heaven (or, increasingly these days, that *all* people will go to Heaven). Naturally we will emphasise the opposite. Because unbelievers think that Christians are smug, 'holier-than-thou' people, it comes as a surprise to them to hear that we define Christians as those who have come to discover that they are hopeless, wretched, lost sinners, who are wholly dependent upon the unfathomable mercy and love of God. The element of surprise enables us to teach the grace of God.

The fact that we believe in judgement, and future punishment in hell, also comes as a great shock. 'Isn't God a God of love?' the surprised unbeliever asks. With his curiosity aroused, we can explain that God is a God of absolute fairness and holiness and justice also, and therefore He must deal with the massive problem of evil. He is pledged to punish sin, and His infinite holiness would destroy any unforgiven sinner who came within the bounds of Heaven.

And why should a holy and infinitely wise God allow sin to pollute the eternal Heaven? Earth is bad enough, with human selfishness, lies, greed and violence, and a wise God would never permit Heaven to be corrupted. Sin must be punished, for God's holiness, justice and wisdom all demand it. There are certain things God cannot do. He cannot fail; He cannot sin; and He cannot be unjust. Only to the curious mind can these truths be effectively explained.

Another matter which quite stuns the completely indifferent unbeliever is the discovery that the Christian's God does not listen to the prayers of most people. The explanation will nearly always be listened to very carefully. What an opportunity we may have to explain that while God may hear *some* prayers offered by non-Christian people in order to encourage them to seek Him, His chief purpose is to save souls, and not to support and bless people in their godless lives.

Prayer must first be made for forgiveness and conversion. It will be heard only if made humbly, by people who yield to the government of the Lord, and who sincerely believe in the atoning death of Christ. How much we can say once a surprised mind is open and listening!

It certainly amazes many people (particularly 'middle-class' people) to discover that we, as Bible-believing Christians, are *against* the ecumenical movement. This is completely puzzling to them and provides a magnificent opportunity for explaining some of the key differences between true and false religion. How much we need to dissociate from phoney ideas about Christianity which have sealed such people in their contempt for the Lord and the Bible!

Some of these approaches may seem a little negative, but they are used as a route to speak gracious and glorious Gospel Truth to the opened mind, as the Lord Himself did. We will not stay long with negative material. We will not dissociate from error in protracted detail. But it is an important and valuable component of our Gospel work, whether in personal witness or preaching.

May the Spirit of God continually help us to learn from our perfect example and teacher, working through us to the blessing of many lost and needy souls in this largest category of all – the ignorant and indifferent.

6. The Self-Righteous Person

THE SELF-RIGHTEOUS category of unbeliever is second in size to that of the ignorant and indifferent. Indeed, the vast majority of people seem to fall into one of these two categories.

Self-righteousness goes back to the excuses made in the Garden of Eden, and has plagued the human race throughout succeeding history. It is interesting to observe that the Lord Jesus Christ dealt with self-righteous people in a broadly similar way, and we can therefore trace a pattern for our own witness.

Self-righteousness is clearly the basis of all 'works' religions, whether Catholicism or any of the world's non-Christian religions and cults, all of which vaunt in some way the individual's capacity to achieve moral excellence and attainment. Self-righteousness is also the basis of proud 'Christian' liberalism which scorns an inspired Bible and the need for atonement and conversion. It is certainly the basis of all nominal Christianity, where people vaguely accept the probability that God is in Heaven, and that Jesus Christ walked on Earth, but feel no great need of personal salvation, and may even be offended at the idea.

Self-righteousness is proud and self-confident. The self-righteous person is satisfied with himself as he is, and usually possesses a sense (even if kept secret) of being superior to the general run of people. Self-righteous people greatly magnify their attributes and good deeds, but minimise, excuse and even ignore their faults.

Before we consider the Saviour's approach to self-righteous people, we need to understand their way of looking at righteousness, as it is so different from the attitude of the Bible-believer. Their idea of righteousness is well illustrated by that of Job's comforters. These men believed that Job was suffering punishment because of some serious, secret iniquity in his life. Not that they felt that anyone should be perfect. To them, *reasonable* righteousness was enough to satisfy God, and this they proudly imagined they had accomplished.

Their theology allowed enormous latitude for self-indulgence, and at the same time gave them scope to pride themselves on being 'righteous'. They did not think for a moment that a holy God required perfection from created beings. That was Job's idea, and it had always irritated them. Indeed, it was this irritation which led them to attack him so furiously when he (according to their way of thinking) came under God's chastisement for sin.

The comforters took the 'schoolmaster' view of God's holy requirements. Eliphaz expressed it in these heavily sarcastic words: 'Shall mortal man be more just than God? shall a man be more pure than his maker? Behold, he put no trust in his servants; and his angels he charged with folly: how much less in them that dwell in houses of clay?' *(Job 4.17-19.)*

Their idea was that God is like the schoolmaster who does not expect his pupils to know as much as he does, or to be as capable. He is extremely pleased if they pass their test with 50%. He is delighted if they achieve 75%, and calls the result a pass with distinction. He certainly does not flog them or expel them for falling short of 100%.

Similarly, according to the comforters, God does not expect perfection from His creatures. Some people are utterly immoral, and they disgust Him. Some achieve a fair degree of self-control. Some score better still (as the comforters imagined they did) and earn the high praise of God, while at the same time being allowed to retain a generous degree of sinful self-indulgence.

That was the proud view of the comforters, and it is

precisely the point of view held by the adherents of false religions, including present-day nominal Christians. It is important to understand their view, if we are to challenge them.

Self-righteous people always underestimate the holiness of God and the seriousness of sin. They pull the mighty God down to their level, while boosting themselves up to His. How did the Lord deal with them? We proceed, first, to His encounter with Nicodemus, recorded in *John 3.*

Nicodemus would inevitably have shared to a great degree the mental outlook of his fellow Jewish leaders in trusting in his own righteousness as sufficient to secure his acceptance by God. The fact that he went to speak with the Lord says something in his favour which cannot be said for his colleagues. To some extent his mind had been opened by the miraculous deeds of Christ.

Whether he wanted to know Christ's 'secret' in order to exploit it personally, or whether he was honestly curious as to how a 'non-establishment' teacher could accomplish such divine wonders, we do not know. However, his mind was at least open to finding out something.

Incidentally, we have in this encounter with Nicodemus a reminder of the enormous significance of our conduct and bearing before unconverted people. It may be that even proud, self-righteous people become intrigued and curious about our Christian faith, as they observe our deportment and behaviour. Because of our handling of various difficult situations, they may be moved to inquire into our church views.

1. Emphasising spiritual experience

Perhaps the most important lesson to learn from our Saviour's encounter with Nicodemus, is the need to emphasise *spiritual experience*. Throughout, the Lord spoke about an experience of new birth, which Nicodemus had never known. It is here that the tender spot of a proud, self-righteous person is best touched, because at this point his spiritual bankruptcy is most obvious.

As soon as we mention the experience of receiving new life and new character (following shame and repentance), the person who evaluates everything in terms of his accomplishments is left floundering. The conversation has turned to something which he has never sought and does not possess.

The witnesser must press on, as the Lord did, to give the clearest possible picture of spiritual new birth. We must draw deeply from our memory store of testimony, both our own, and the testimonies of friends, family and colleagues, or fragments drawn from Christian biography, to illustrate the point. The new birth is the one thing that the self-righteous person cannot claim to have attained to, or to be good at, and this is therefore the issue which we must continually stress.

Note, once more, the element of surprise in Christ's words – 'Except a man be born again, he cannot see the kingdom of God.' Nicodemus, the religious leader, was given no saving credit at all for his life of meticulous ceremonial law-keeping. No doubt the Lord's tone was kindly and gracious, but the absolute necessity of a great spiritual crisis was presented as the only way to God.

We must learn to speak about the new birth, and to describe the nature of this great change, so magnificently pictured by the birth of a baby, with all its new faculties. We must show that no one can give rise to his own birth, but the imparting of spiritual life and change is something which only God can do for us.

Some writers of hyper-Calvinistic bent have drawn on this passage of Scripture as though the Lord gave a theological lecture on the entire spiritual work of salvation in a soul. They say (as we described earlier in this book) that the new birth (regeneration) opens the eyes of a person and from that moment he is a fully-fledged, converted believer. In their view the only value of Christ's testimony to Nicodemus was to knock down his human pride. They fail to see in Christ's words any personal appeal to Nicodemus to repent, or any 'offer' of salvation.

We take a very different view of the passage. We do not see it as a wholly negative lecture on the regenerating work of the Spirit, but as a powerful challenge leading to a touching appeal to the heart. The birth illustration in this passage may be taken in its fulness as a description of conversion. Just as human birth begins with conception and proceeds through nine months of gestation before resulting in visible birth, so conversion begins with the implanting of life (regeneration) and proceeds through the awakening of a soul, conviction of sin, repentance and belief, culminating in conscious birth. Only after repentance and faith is the seeker in conscious possession of new spiritual faculties, and assurance.

The Saviour did not speak to Nicodemus merely to humble and crush him and leave him in despair. He spoke to alarm his soul, and to educate him about his need of Holy Ghost conversion, and we must do the same. We must speak in the hope that the Spirit of God will work, and that our words will be used by Him as He brings people to embrace Christ willingly.

Christ went on to speak of the descent from Heaven to earth of the 'Son of man', of how He must be 'lifted up' (as the brazen serpent had been) so that those who trust only in Him 'should not perish, but have eternal life'. Then the Lord uttered the magnificent words of the 'universal tender of the Gospel' to all who believe (John 3.16).

The key point to remember in this encounter is the emphasis on the necessity of personal conversion. Such an emphasis is the best way of discomforting and stirring self-righteous people. This is where they are at their weakest. They desperately lack true spiritual experience.

2. Making matters personal

As we prepare to speak to those who are self-righteous we may wonder how we will get on if a debate develops. Will we be outmanoeuvred? By virtue of His divine wisdom the Saviour could have defeated anyone in debate, but instead of overpowering His opponents with numerous invincible arguments, He held to one crucial point, which He would present by means of apt and moving illustrations. And in the case of self-righteous people, He usually made matters personal. We see this in the encounter with Nicodemus. Within a short time, the Lord applied His message personally saying, '*Ye* must be born again.'

The parable of the Good Samaritan was given during the course of a debate with a wily and self-righteous scholar of Jewish law *(Luke 10.25-37)*. The lawyer began by 'tempting' the Lord with the question – 'What shall I do to inherit eternal life?' It may be that he hoped Christ's answer would reveal a departure from orthodoxy.

The lawyer would certainly have shared the theological views of the rest of the religious establishment, and would have trusted in his own righteousness. As the text tells us, his question was not sincere, and he clearly did not think he had anything to learn.

These are the chief features of all self-righteous people. They do not want to learn anything from witnessing Christians. They know all they want to know. They are among the most unteachable people in the world. Interestingly, we observe that the Lord did not immediately attempt to teach the lawyer anything. Unlike us, He did not launch into a lecture, but 'parried' the lawyer's question with another. 'He said unto him, What is written in the law? how readest thou?'

In witness, we do not have to rush to answer when asked a question. Sometimes it does not pay to answer too quickly. The person to whom we are witnessing may be trying to lure us along some line of discussion which we will later regret. It always pays to think for a moment about what lies behind the question, and to answer the question with another question. We should want to know a little more about a person's views and how he looks at the things of God before we decide what approach to take.

We realise that the Saviour did not ask His question because He needed more information. He knew the answer already. He put His question in order to lay a finger on the lawyer's soul, and we may have to do the same when dealing with self-righteous people. The issue may need to be made *very personal* early in our witness.

The lawyer gave a good reply. He said – 'Thou shalt love the Lord thy God with all thy heart, and with all thy soul, and with all thy strength, and with all thy mind; and thy neighbour as thyself.' But this good reply led him into deeper water, for the Lord Jesus responded with words which implied that the lawyer had never accomplished this. He said: 'Thou hast answered right: this do, and thou shalt live.'

What could the lawyer say to this? As an eminent member of the religious hierarchy, he now found himself in a position where it had been publicly suggested that he did not love and serve God as he should, and that he had progress to make. At the very least he had been made to look foolish, as if he did not know the answer to a very simple question. Would he say, 'But I already do all these things!' and perhaps appear conceited in the eyes of the onlookers? Or would he let the rather humiliating implication of Christ's words go unchallenged?

He had to decide whether to claim righteousness, or by his silence to acknowledge failure. There was only one way out of his dilemma, and he took it. He quibbled over words.

Clearly we cannot imitate the divine expertise of the Lord in producing this kind of position within seconds. But we can learn from this that our objective should be to make the self-righteous person face up to his position. He must not be allowed to air his knowledge, wallow in his boasts and disdain evangelical Truth. We have to lay a finger on his soul and help him to realise that his heart is naked before God.

The lawyer, to escape from the trap, and in order to justify himself, asked the question: 'Who is my neighbour?' The result was that he found himself listening to a captivating parable of the hardness and hypocrisy of the human heart, even in men who claimed to be highly religious. This leads us to the next point to be emphasised in witnessing to self-righteous people.

3. Emphasising the sins of the heart

The parable of the good Samaritan provides a perfect example of how to deal with those plagued by a self-righteous spirit. It also includes a particularly provocative element calculated to arouse the attention of the listener. Confronted by an audience including many leaders of the religious establishment, the Lord portrayed the Jewish clergy as hard-hearted hypocrites, and selected a Samaritan as hero of the day. This was an obvious use of shock tactics, given the contempt of Jews for Samaritans. In this parable diplomacy was sacrificed to achieve the greatest cutting edge for the Truth.

So the Lord again distanced Himself from the religious errors of the Jewish leaders in order to teach that true godliness does not spring from ceremonial observance, or outward matters, but from the *heart* and *character* of a person. Thus a Samaritan, regarded by them as unthinkably unclean, emerged as the one who showed true godliness.

Just as the heartlessness and pride of the self-righteous priestly community was exposed by Christ, so today we must demolish the hopelessly inadequate concept of righteousness which makes the self-righteous person so satisfied with himself. The Jewish leaders focused on *external* conduct such as services, washings, fastings, sacrifices, and details of clothing, all the while ignoring the heart sins, such as pride, selfishness, deceit, mental greed and lusting.

We must be ready to talk about *heart sins* as the deep-seated perversions which make everyone guilty, hopeless and offensive to Almighty God. These are the sins which are forgotten by self-righteous people. Outward deeds they may sometimes acknowledge, but their inward *condition* of sin, to this they are blind.

We must tell self-righteous people that true character starts *within.* God sees the state of our hearts. What matters is not outward cultural advantages, affectations or veneers of courtesy, but inner motives and desires.

Of course, the hardest things which have to be said to self-righteous people will need to be reserved for preaching. Personal witness speaks directly to the individual, but to strongly and directly challenge and expose all the sins of the heart could be deeply offensive and potentially explosive. It is certainly not practical to mount this level of witness to one's employer.

Sometimes it is better to give the hardest challenges by way of a book or booklet, or, if possible, by bringing a person under the sound of Gospel preaching. Preaching, as we so frequently point out, is a stroke of divine genius, for by addressing many people it avoids personal offence. It is therefore able to describe most fully the state and need of the human heart.

As far as personal witness is concerned, the best approach for us is to make use of parables such as the one we shall refer to in these pages. By telling and explaining these we can speak in the 'third person', and keep our witness within the bounds of courtesy, yet without forfeiting clarity.

Our Lord's example with self-righteous people tells us that the ultimate aim of our witness is to show that God judges them not according to how they imagine themselves to be, but according to the real condition of their hearts. How will today's self-righteous people stand on the day of judgement when the secrets of all hearts are revealed?

As we have noted, the self-righteous person boosts himself up in his own estimation, and if he believes in God at all, he pulls God down to his puny level. In imagining that God will be pleased with him he attributes to God his own superficial standards. Thus he adds to his personal conceit the sin of insulting and degrading Almighty God. By some means, perhaps gently at first, he must be shown what he is doing. We need to emphasise that it is impossible to know God or to go to Heaven without sincere repentance and conversion (due to His infinite holiness and purity).

The New Testament is never flattering to self-righteousness. We remember how John the Baptist called the scribes and Pharisees 'a brood of vipers'. Obviously we cannot use such language in our witness, but it reminds us that our witness must aim a spotlight on the *heart*s of people.

In the viper illustration of John, self-righteous people are described as having a great deal of cunning. They are schemers. Very many are highly possessive and covetous, always calculating and planning for the things which serve their own interests. They are very proud people whose minds work overtime justifying their conduct and reviewing the 'evidence' for their imagined superiority over others. These are the heart sins.

Possessiveness and self-seeking go hand in hand with self-righteousness. The element of cunning condemned by John the Baptist arises because self-righteous people wish to indulge their self-seeking ways and at the same time convince themselves and others that they are fine and admirable people.

They hide their strategies and schemes in the long

grass of gushing charm and double-talk – hence the snake analogy. They can literally ooze with affected warmth and kindness, but really they are motivated by entirely self-centred considerations.

Middle-class society is generously endowed with self-righteousness. It can put on an impressive 'front' of decency, respectability and friendliness, but under-neath there is so often a seething cauldron. The heart decides everything on the basis of – 'How will this affect me? What will it do for my reputation? Am I being treated as I ought to be?'

Self-righteous people are out to put on a good show; to do better than (or at least as well as) the neighbours; to press their children through university solely for the sake of parental prestige, and so forth. Other people (even their family) are sometimes mere pawns in their self-flattering schemes.

For this reason the self-righteous person needs to have a kind of explosive charge detonated to lay bare the heart. Someone has to stress that God looks upon those heart sins – covetousness, possessiveness, jeal-ousy, pride and self-interest.

We stress again that in these areas personal witness *must* co-operate with preaching because it is easier for preaching to say the hard and personal things.

In *Luke 11.37-44* we see how the Lord Jesus dealt with a proud Pharisee with whom He went to dine: 'And as he spake, a certain Pharisee besought him to dine with him: and he went in, and sat down to meat. And when the Pharisee saw it, he marvelled that he had not first washed before dinner.'

Of course the Lord did not *forget* to wash. He omitted the procedure quite deliberately, even provocatively, and said to His host: 'Now do ye Pharisees make clean the outside of the cup and the platter; but your inward part is full of ravening and wickedness.'

Clearly our Lord's procedure here is not intended as an exact pattern for us to follow. He was, after all, the Lord of Glory and could see into this Pharisee's heart. He possessed perfect knowledge and sovereign authority to be able to speak as He did. We must not be so blunt so early, especially when a guest in someone's house!

Nevertheless, we learn from our Saviour's words what our *objective* should be, even if our procedure must be careful, slow and gentle. The Lord's strategy was to destroy the fabric of the Pharisee's self-satisfaction, which lay in *external* behaviour. The Saviour turned the spotlight on *internal* behaviour; the *heart* sins.

Quite often we have the opportunity to make these points in a general and detached manner. When there is a discussion about religion we may be able to launch into the theme that the Lord looks upon the heart when He evaluates people. We do not have to make direct accusations or remarks about any self-righteous person who may be the 'target' of our message. We can approach the subject in general terms.

We can point out in a dispassionate way that inner appetites, pride, deceit, and so forth are the disfigurations which make us offensive to God, and make us appear 'wretched, and miserable, and poor, and blind, and naked' in His holy sight. This emphasis was certainly that of the Lord, as seen in His words: 'Woe unto you, scribes and Pharisees, hypocrites! for ye are as graves which appear not, and the men that walk over them are not aware of them' *(Luke 11.44)*. They looked fine as they preened themselves in religious finery. But just as people could not see the state of the rotting corpses buried beneath their feet, so the hearts behind the religious robes were to God's view full of corruption.

4. Exposing petty niceties

In addition to teaching the contrast between external righteousness and heart sins, there is another distinction which the self-righteous person must be shown. He needs to be shown how God distinguishes between *minor* matters and *major* matters, because the self-righteous person evaluates his performance in terms of lesser niceties. He is so often concerned with matters of culture and refinement, such as whether one knows how to say please or thank you, and whether one has the right social graces. This is certainly not to suggest that good manners are unimportant, but, as we know, they do not count for eternal salvation.

The Lord aimed this particular arrow of conviction at the hearts of self-righteous Pharisees in these words: 'Woe unto you, Pharisees! for ye tithe mint and rue and all manner of herbs, and pass over judgment and the love of God' *(Luke 11.42)*.

Self-righteous people today feel superior even over matters of dress-sense, decor and taste. They are deeply concerned about money, status, and even accents. The list of peripheral and external shibboleths is almost endless. But God requires humility, meekness, love, concern for others, separation from evil, unselfishness and, above all, love, loyalty and obedience to Himself and His cause. The self-righteous person knows nothing of these things and must be brought to realise that in God's sight he is, (a) a proud, deluded 'externalist', and (b) a fanatic for the trivial, and therefore a neglecter of all truly important values.

5. *Exposing contrived 'righteousness' which is just for show*

The Lord put His finger on yet another major fault with this class of unbeliever when He said, 'Woe unto you, Pharisees! for ye love the uppermost seats in the synagogues, and greetings in the markets' *(Luke 11.43)*. He showed that even their external works were maintained chiefly to impress those who noticed them. All their imagined 'righteousness' was performed for watching eyes! They were not capable of genuine and sincere decency, righteousness or charity. They were not moved by their consciences, which were virtually dead, but by their love of reputation.

So today, self-righteousness turns on its charming, courteous face for the guests, but this demeanour changes very quickly once the guests are gone. The 'righteousness' and 'qualities' are merely a play-act. When the audience has gone, the snapping, ungracious churl reappears.

How quickly the middle classes of Britain abandoned the external pretence of high moral standards when the 'new morality' of the 1960s appeared, and it became apparent that the old values were no longer admired and respected by society in general! What was the point of maintaining behaviour which no one any longer applauded?

We remember the Lord's words about the Pharisees – 'Take heed that ye do not your alms before men, to be seen of them . . .' *(Matthew 6.1)*. As the Lord said, they sounded a trumpet before they did their righteous deeds, and prayed standing at the corners of the streets. They revealed in their deportment all the symptoms of self-righteousness, with all its love of admiring eyes and reputation. To do the right thing out of a sincere heart, and to live in order to please God, was not their way.

6. Dismantling comparative righteousness

In the parable of the Pharisee and the publican the Saviour exposed the technique by which self-righteous people boost their delusion of moral decency and good nature. And today, in our preaching and witness, we shall need to expose this also. *Luke 18.9* records how He spoke to 'certain which trusted in themselves that they were righteous, and despised others', telling them the parable of the Pharisee and the publican. This is a perfect parable for weaving into our witness.

The Lord showed here how self-righteous people engage in the trick of *comparative righteousness*. They convince themselves of their fine performance and character by comparing themselves, not with good people, but with those who have many obvious faults, and who are moral and social failures. The Pharisee in the parable spotted in the Temple a publican who had committed certain sins which he, the Pharisee, had not committed. Immediately he began to wallow in self-congratulation, while he denigrated the publican.

All self-righteous people employ this method. They are snobby, critical and fault-finding in all kinds of ways. Every sneer and criticism is another rung on the ladder of self-elevation. Christ's parable is designed to bring them down in real self-awareness.

The self-righteous hearers of Christ's day were shocked by the outcome of this parable, for the

Pharisee stood condemned, and the repentant publican emerged as the one who had standing with God. (Once again the Lord used the element of the unexpected to surprise listeners, and to impress His lesson upon their minds.)

The Lord showed that the prayers of the self-righteous are not heard because they are proud, they do not ask for forgiveness, and they exclude *heart* sins from their thinking. God particularly hates pride, and will not deal with pompous and haughty people who bask in self-esteem.

The personal pronoun 'I' occurs five times in the Pharisee's short prayer (though it is more of a boast than a prayer). How typical of the self-righteous!

7. Exposing bondage to ego and possessions

The case of the rich young ruler *(Luke 18.18-27)* sheds further light on how we must approach the self-righteous. Luke tells us that 'a certain ruler asked him, saying, Good Master, what shall I do to inherit eternal life?' The Lord first questioned this man about the second table of the law. In reply, he showed his grossly superficial view of sin by claiming to have kept all those commandments. Interpreted in the most narrow sense, it is possible that he had kept them. But this is the problem with self-righteous people. Standards are always interpreted in the narrowest possible way.

The young man may have been clear of physical

adultery, but what about lust? He had not killed, but was he guilty of hatred, rage, malice or unkindness? He had not actually stolen, but what of extortion, taking advantage, underpaying his employees, and so on? He had not falsely charged anyone with a crime, but what about lies, excuses, slander and backbiting?

As Ryle says of this young man, 'An answer more full of darkness and self-ignorance it is impossible to conceive! He who made it could have known nothing, either about himself, or God, or God's law.' Such is the condition of all self-righteous people.

The Lord's main challenge came when He put His finger on the young ruler's greatest defect and sin – his bondage to the dictates of ego, and to his possessions. His twin gods were his exalted position in society, and his riches. When the Saviour invited him to sell everything he possessed and follow Him, the young man could not do it. He would have followed Christ, in his own way, only if it had been possible for him to keep his shrine and idols – his ego and possessions.

If only we could show self-righteous people their bondage! If only we could prick that balloon of complacent superiority and self-satisfaction! And to some extent we can, by using this searching account in our explanation of true conversion. Here is a picture of people who will not yield to Christ – and why not? Because they are held in the clutches of pride and self-service, and cannot break their hold.

Patiently but clearly we must convey just this to self-righteous people. Their lives bring nothing at all to the true God, but they are the poor slaves of two gods – their own egos, and this material world.

8. Exposing hatred of repentance

The final ingredient of our message to the self-righteous is the most difficult, and we may well consider this matter best left to the preacher. *Matthew 21.33-44* records the vineyard parable, which speaks of a householder who 'planted a vineyard, and hedged it round about, and digged a winepress in it, and built a tower, and let it out to husbandmen, and went into a far country.'

The husbandmen, or tenant farmers, decided to seize the vineyard for themselves, and to beat, stone and kill the various messengers who were sent to collect the owner's dues. When at last the owner sent his son, 'they said among themselves, This is the heir; come, let us kill him, and let us seize on his inheritance.' And they slew the son.

The lord of the vineyard destroyed the wicked husbandmen and let his vineyard out to others, and the Saviour concluded the parable with these solemn words: 'Did ye never read in the scriptures, The stone which the builders rejected, the same is become the head of the corner: this is the Lord's doing, and it is marvellous in our eyes? Therefore say I unto you, The

115

kingdom of God shall be taken from you, and given to a nation bringing forth the fruits thereof.' It is recorded that 'when the chief priests and Pharisees had heard his parables, they perceived that he spake of them.' This parable was plainly directed against the self-righteous leaders of the Jewish people, and its purpose is to present God's analysis of self-righteousness.

Righteousness is described in terms of a vineyard – the vineyard of righteousness. It is God's property and territory, but the self-righteous have seized it and occupied it. They have no right to be there and they pay no dues to God. They are not legitimate occupants, and worse, they reject all God's overtures to them to inaugurate a right relationship. Even though God sends His Son to make it possible for them to live in the vineyard of righteousness, they say – 'No! Let us take Him and kill Him.'

The self-righteous are squatters in God's territory. They want to appear as upright, decent people, but they reject the terms. They are intruders, and they are unclean. They will not enter the territory through the gate which is provided, and they hate and harm anyone (including witnessing Christians) who poses a threat to their occupation of this ground.

The self-righteous person must be shown that if he maintains his pretence (his imagined righteousness), and rejects the message of an atoning Saviour, then he will eventually be dealt with as a trespasser who has seized and stolen a territory. It is significant that in this parable the Lord indicates that the intruder *knows what he is doing* when he wilfully spurns the message of mercy and grace.

The theme of our message to the self-righteous must therefore be: 'No repentance – no conversion. No repentance – no Heaven and no hope. No repentance – no escape from the day when rebels must stand condemned before the Judge of all the earth.'

The Lord declared to Chorazin and Bethsaida that they would fare worse than Tyre and Sidon in the day of judgement. The middle-class cities of that 'religious' nation were stripped of all their imagined righteousness by the Lord. What was wrong with Chorazin and Bethsaida? What was wrong with Capernaum? Their great sin was that they had found a way to avoid repenting. They told themselves that they were righteous already, and therefore did not need to repent.

7. The Self-Interested Person

THERE IS A CLASS of unbeliever which needs particular care in these days, because it appears to be easy to reach, comes to faith quickly, and supplies numerous new members to the churches of Christ. But the outcome ranges from disappointment to disaster. Converts from this category either fall back into the world fairly soon, or remain longer to give untold trouble. This is the 'self-interested' category of unbeliever.

People in this category may be quite humble, self-effacing people. They are not at all like the self-righteous, proud Pharisees, or the general run of ignorant and indifferent people. Their openness and apparent sincerity appeals to us, and we naturally form high expectations that they will find the Lord.

We do not detect, at first, that they are only interested in Christianity because they have seen something which they like or want for themselves. Nevertheless, they are attracted by something other than the need for pardon and reconciliation with God, whether they realise it or not.

1. Emphasising real conviction and repentance

During His earthly ministry the Lord Jesus took pains to rebuff with solemn warnings all who tried to follow Him in a superficial way, without having first understood the way of true repentance and the cost of discipleship. Several passages in the Gospels show how Christ dealt with this type of hearer, and we must learn from His example.

If we are determined to make the spiritual aspects of the Gospel clear to the 'easy volunteer', then we will undoubtedly be used by God to bring some to genuine repentance. Vast numbers of truly converted people first came to church out of self-interest. Today, they bless God that those who witnessed to them and befriended them were determined to make them see the *real* issues of repentance and conversion.

There is hope for the self-interested person, because the Holy Spirit can change the leopard's spots. But we must be faithful with the Gospel, or people with only a meaningless, superficial profession of faith will enter into the churches out of self-interest.

The self-interested class of unbeliever is possibly slightly on the increase at the present time, judging from the success of certain church growth techniques which focus on giving people what they want. Strategies which shamelessly mix a morsel of Gospel with an abundance of entertainment, worldliness, companionship and pleasure are attracting large numbers of 'outsiders' into churches and house-groups, indicating the presence of a huge market of self-interested people.

In the parable of the sower this class is portrayed by the thin film of fertile soil which covers the outcrop of rock. In this soil the seed is likely to spring up readily, but the root of the matter will not be there.

In days of decadence, when real blessing is small, even the most careful Gospel workers are vulnerable to being over-impressed by people who make a ready response to their testimony. A positive response is so unusual that we tend to assume that a deep work of God is being carried out in every heart. But what if people are self-interested, and have only become interested in our message for reasons of earthly and personal benefit?

What if such people accept all we tell them, learn the language of Zion, and join the local church? Soon they will be a thorn in our side, and may continue as such for years to come. It has often been said that most of the difficulties which churches experience are due to the presence of unconverted people in their

120

membership. Some pastors complain of members who grumble, groan, pout, grimace, and show no enthusiasm whatever for spiritual things or for evangelism. Instead they inflame any and every difficulty which comes along.

It is unfortunate, perhaps, that these dubious members do not become theological liberals, denying the faith and thus exposing themselves to censure or discipline. Many manage to linger on in churches all their lives, just staying the right side of the 'law', but always proving a trial to godly pastors and workers. Our concern as preachers and witnessing Christians must be to avoid introducing another generation of such people if we can possibly help it.

Mass evangelistic crusades are probably the main culprits for canvassing and enlisting self-interested people, then rushing them into making professions before they have time to think what they are doing. Not that mass evangelism is intrinsically wrong, but in modern times it has usually featured a shallow Gospel presentation, coupled with a 'commercial' need to produce numerous instant converts.*

If millions attend Catholic churches, liberal churches and cult meeting-places out of self-interest, we should

---

*See *Seven Certain Signs of True Conversion*, subtitled, *A guide to the marks of true conversion for those who doubt their salvation, and for the use of spiritual counsellors,* a Sword & Trowel booklet.

not imagine, as evangelicals, that we shall be immune from such adherents.

2. Avoiding earthly incentives

The longest chapter of John's Gospel (having 71 verses) is devoted to showing how the Lord dealt with people who followed Him for the wrong reasons. *John 6.2* sets the scene: 'And a great multitude followed him, because they saw his miracles which he did on them that were diseased.'

These people flocked after the Lord. They seemed ready to listen and went to great lengths to track Him down. Yet the chapter shows that most of them had no interest in spiritual information, nor any inclination to repent of their sin. They saw other things which interested them.

Some of them wanted to see spectacular miracles. Others wanted to see this miracle-worker assume power as a national leader, fulfilling no doubt the Jewish longing for someone who would rid them of the Roman army of occupation, and revitalise their national fortunes *(John 6.15)*.

They wanted exciting events to enter into their dreary lives. They did not have television sets, cinemas, nor all the other things that worldlings depend upon today. To them, this great orator and miraculous provider of bread was the most exciting prospect in Israel for many generations.

However, the Lord did not encourage this unenlightened enthusiasm, as some mistakenly do today. (Nowadays, for example, the charismatics use healing and prosperity as baits to attract adherents.) The Lord faced people with their true motives, and if they made no progress in a spiritual direction, He actually put them off. By the end of *John 6*, we read that, 'Many of his disciples went back, and walked no more with him' (verse 66). This was the result of our Lord's warnings to them. When faced with superficial interest the Lord put it to the test and questioned it. He made the terms of discipleship so° clear that only people with a° real spiritual concern for repentance and life continued to follow Him.

3. *True faith is more than intellectual enthusiasm*

John's Gospel records a number of qualities which self-interested people may appear to possess, so that we should not be caught out. They may at first possess a strong degree of seemingly genuine belief in the things of God, yet still fall far short of evangelical repentance and obedience. *John 6.14* records: 'Then those men, when they had seen the miracle that Jesus did, said, This is of a truth that prophet that should come into the world.' They believed the prophecies about a coming Messiah, and accepted that the Lord's miracles were accomplished by divine power.

The superficial person may accept the Word of God and the divinity of Christ and yet remain totally self-interested. He may attend church, mentally accept the message and appear to be enthusiastic about the atmosphere of evangelistic services. He may seem very open to our every word in private witness, but he may be of the same ilk as those who, at the end, 'walked no more with him'.

Some years ago a brilliant speaker and writer in the field of Christian apologetic reasoning gained a tremendous following in the universities of America and Europe. The skill and strength of his arguments attracted huge numbers of students and other young people to the Christian faith. However, these enthusiastic 'converts' mostly tended to slip back into their worldly ways once they left their university environment.

The man at the centre of all this made a solidly reformed and powerful contribution to the field of evangelistic literature, but his following soon peaked and faded. Why did those young people not continue in their profession? The answer is that this era of brilliant apologetic evangelism happened to coincide with a period during which students had become disenchanted with materialistic philosophy. Many people wanted something intellectually stimulating with which to challenge the greedy, self-seeking society around them. They wanted some explanation for the state of society, and they found it in an engaging presentation of evangelical apologetics.

Tragically, it would appear that most did not experience conviction of sin, sincere repentance and the new birth. They looked only for something impressive and fresh for their minds. They were in the 'self-interested' class; the thin layer of soil lying on rocky ground. They were those who, for a time, believed the message, though not for the right reasons, and soon fell away.

What does the hearer of the Gospel want? Is it something for the mind only? Or is it something for the heart only, such as companionship and friendship and love?

4. The folly of 'need-based' evangelism

John 6.24 warns us that false discipleship can be accompanied by apparent zeal, effort and sacrifice: 'When the people therefore saw that Jesus was not there, neither his disciples, they also took shipping, and came to Capernaum, seeking for Jesus.'

But the Lord told them that they sought Him because they had received a good meal. They had not even been *rightly* impressed by the miracle! Their response was not like that of Simon Peter who, when he saw a great miracle, fell on his knees and said, 'Depart from me; for I am a sinful man, O Lord.'

In the course of our witness we may be over-impressed by someone who goes to some lengths to meet us for spiritual conversation, or to attend church. We experience so many disappointments and broken promises that any concerned hearer appears to be genuine. But such a person may still turn out to be self-interested, and we must therefore keep the basic message of 'repentance and remission of sins' well to the fore.

Some people are ready to listen because they want some spiritual security. Others just want companionship and feel they may find it in a church. A number of people who have church-going backgrounds may feel comfortable maintaining a measure of worship. It may give them some kind of inner peace. Often people with an evangelical upbringing drift back to the atmosphere and environment in which they feel 'at home'. Then there are people who merely want to consolidate their self-righteousness by a degree of church attendance.

Nowadays we find evangelists who pander to self-interest to secure attention. We hear of 'need-based' evangelism, which offers happiness to the sad, companionship to the lonely, counselling and restoration to those in marital difficulties, recreation to the bored, and so on. But if we bait and lure people by offering whatever it may be that they desire, we must not be surprised to discover, in the end, that our 'converts' are sadly deluded, self-interested people.

This may seem very negative and depressing to contemplate, but we must always be ready to recognise when there is no meaningful desire for repentance and spiritual experience in a person.

For the self-interested, we must follow the example of *John 6* and make it absolutely plain that we bring a message of spiritual conversion. It was when the Lord stressed the *spiritual* purpose of His coming that they began to murmur and question everything He said.

The Lord warned: 'Labour not for the meat which perisheth, but for that meat which endureth unto everlasting life, which the Son of man shall give unto you' *(John 6.27)*. Following this, we read of the deepening perplexity of the crowd, as their minds struggled with, and refused, the message of atonement and the need for *spiritual* life.

'This is the work of God,' said Christ, 'that ye believe on him whom he hath sent.' Belief, as opposed to works, was stressed; a humbling message which called attention to people's spiritual bankruptcy, inadequacy, sinfulness and failure.

5. Stressing the new life and the lordship of Christ

The self-interested person wants something in this life, but our message emphasises an emergency situation of spiritual and eternal loss, unless all our interests in this life are renounced in favour of Christ and the gift of salvation.

If the normal conversation of an interested person is

about earthly things, we will be on our guard. If there are no doubts and fears, no spiritual problems (only intellectual ones), then we will be cautious.

Other passages show how the Saviour cautioned people who were self-confident and self-interested. We think of two of the men whose approach to Him is recorded in *Luke 9.57-62.* These possessed an apparent interest in Christ's teaching and works, and pressed themselves upon Him, saying, 'Lord, I will follow thee.' But it was clear to the Lord that they did not grasp what they were doing, and were full of self-interest. He therefore confronted them with the cost of discipleship. He told them that they must live by faith and cut their former ties.

We, too, must make clear that our message is one of conversion, which involves dying to self and to the old life, and living entirely for Christ. No longer is the convert preoccupied with his future, his interests, his career, his earthly happiness, his security, and so on. He now lives for the Lord and His cause.

This was in the mind of the Lord when He said, 'So likewise, whosoever he be of you that forsaketh not all that he hath, he cannot be my disciple' *(Luke 14.33).* The Lord does not want us to rush people into making quick professions of faith.

When Jacob returned home, terrified of meeting Esau, he prayed earnestly for God to deliver him. But the Lord acted as though to say, 'This time, Jacob, you must really mean it.' And so God withstood Jacob, wrestling with him, so that he struggled and laboured in earnest prayer before receiving the blessing. In a way, this is what God requires of the self-interested seeker. He must be told, kindly but firmly, that there is no hope of conversion until the Lord is approached for the right reasons, on the right terms, and with genuine repentance and yielding to Christ's lordship.

In this connection we must be careful in our churches of the 'YPF syndrome'. Many fellowships enjoy the presence of a dedicated and energetic youth leader who is able to gather a group of teenagers into regular meetings. Often these include regular recreational activities. The trouble is that those who lead the work, well motivated though they may be, frequently overlook the self-interest in the human heart. It is an observable fact that often the majority of the members of such a teenage group will profess Christ, and yet most will have 'rebelled' or fallen away before they reach their twenties.

The passing of a few years will show that one or two maintain a good stand, and one or two more have lingered on as rather unsatisfactory church members, but most discard their brief profession of Christ.

The reason for the poor record of youth groups is that young people will readily accept the religious message of a group which provides companionship and security. These things are of great importance to the young, and they will be strongly inclined to identify with and profess all that the group stands for, partly to please, and partly to secure full acceptance. They will probably not be conscious of these motives, but they will be there.

Most young people will even undergo some form of emotional experience as they accept the message, and in the short term this may be hard to distinguish from true conversion. If only there were less recreation, and more of the spiritual message in such groups, the problem of spurious professions might be more avoidable. If only the leaders would concentrate less energy on the same few youngsters, and more on reaching a larger number, the peer-group danger might be less significant. If only the young people were encouraged to attend regular Gospel ministry with the main congregation, the problem might also be less acute.

A greater awareness of the self-interest which lurks in the heads of many unconverted people, young and old, would deliver us from many snares in our Gospel work. In personal witness, this class of unbeliever needs to have particularly emphasised the self-renouncing and spiritual aspects of true conversion. This was the example of our Great Physician.

It is only as we stick firmly to our emphasis on repentance, turning away from the world, and yielding to the lordship of Christ, that we shall minister true blessing to those in the grip of human self-interest.

8. The Convinced Atheist

IN DAYS WHEN PEOPLE have for so long been bombarded by materialism and rationalistic influences, we must expect a vast increase in the number of convinced atheists. The older writers dubbed this class of unbeliever 'proud infidels', a term which drew attention to the atheist's feeling of superiority at having rejected God.

Charles Bridges distinguished between the *sensual infidel*, the *imitative infidel*, and the *shrewd infidel*. The sensual atheist rejects God out of lust. His 'god is his belly'. He hates the idea that he is observed by a holy God.

The imitative atheist goes along with the God-rejecting crowd because it is the fashionable thing to do, and because he will not think for himself.

In the case of the shrewd atheist, says Bridges, 'we find the love of sin gathering strength from the pride of reasoning.'

Atheists are not to be confused with ignorant and indifferent people. The latter may vaguely believe in the existence of God, even though they give the matter no further thought. Atheists are those who have thought about the matter and have decided to expel the recognition of God from their minds altogether. They will argue the point, and many welcome every opportunity to do so.

1. Avoiding mere intellectual argument

The root cause of atheism is expressed by the Lord in *John 3.19-20*: 'And this is the condemnation, that light is come into the world, and men loved darkness rather than light, because their deeds were evil. For every one that doeth evil hateth the light, neither cometh to the light, lest his deeds should be reproved.'

Three crucial facts are taught in these words. The first is that *sin is the basis of atheism*. The second is that *fear of reproof* leads people to avoid the mention of God. They cannot stand the pangs of conscience. The third is that *proud independence hates light*, that is, instruction and guidance from outside self.

Love of sin, then, is the prime motive for adopting atheistic views. People reject the existence of God because they want to indulge their pride and be free to do what they like. The atheist gains (so he thinks) tremendous liberation the moment he repudiates the restraints of a God-ordained moral system.

Here is the real motive underlying the attitude of the atheist. First and foremost he is determined to be unhindered and uninhibited in the conduct of his life. He wants to be morally free to follow the dictates of his heart, his ambitions, his opinions and his whims. He may well adopt some cultural refinements and a moral system of his own if it suits his purpose. But all his intellectual objections to God are produced from a mind acting under orders from the heart, where lusts reign.

The second fact taught in Christ's words is that the atheist has come to his position because he hates the pangs of conscience. He positions himself as far away as he can from God-given standards because he cannot bear a single stab of shame, accusation or awareness of his fallen ways. One of the chief purposes of his atheism is to protect himself from the movings of conscience.

The third fact taught by the Lord about the atheist is that he is proud, and does not want to be dependent upon God for anything. He does not want to feel indebted to God for life, help or grace, nor does he want to obey Him in anything. He likes to think that he is competent, self-sufficient and capable. The idea of being a dependent being offends his ego. He wants to be the master of his life; the captain of his ship. He will *not* be a mere servant of God.

These three factors are all matters of the *heart* rather than of the *head,* and while the atheist must have his intellectual unbelief challenged, his real problem is a moral one, namely – rebellion. And the rebellion is seen in the three symptoms described by the Lord – sinful behaviour, hatred of conscience, and pride. We will therefore be doing the worst thing if we flatter an atheist's intellectual objections, treat them as reasonable, and enter into long discussions on apologetic themes, struggling to prove God by rational argument.

2. Exposing the folly and consequences of sin

We must approach convinced atheists in a way which takes account of the Lord's analysis of their unbelief. As they love sin, and value above all else their liberty to please themselves, and do what they like, we may emphasise the suffering and squalor which results from such an outlook.

This approach is also appropriate for another part of Christ's analysis, namely, the pride and independence of atheists. They partly reject God because they pride themselves that they, and the human race, are self-sufficient. They must believe in the inevitable rise and progress of the human race, and the lofty power of the human mind.

The exposing of the ravages of sin in the world

effectively ridicules and rebukes the absurdities of human pride, and also the utter foolishness of the love of sin. Atheists love and defend sin. They imagine people are essentially good and trustworthy, and they hate what they call the 'nanny society'. They think society will work without moral restraints. We, therefore, will speak about the miserable failure of the human race, and about its weakness, wretchedness, unkindness and hostility. The hopeless plight of mankind hits very hard at the atheist's policy because it shouts to the roof-tops the depravity built into the human make-up.

So we should stress the fact that people are impotent to improve themselves or to conquer their problems while in their state of rebellion against God, and the biblical moral system.

The disorder which prevails at personal, family, national and international levels cries out against the atheist's theory that people have power to make progress and order their affairs aright. Humanity's problems are a great blow to the pride of the atheist.

Isaiah 5 is a magnificent example of *moral* reasoning with atheists. Here God, through the prophet, remonstrates with the Jews (the vineyard of the Lord) for whom He had done everything possible, and to whom He had given great privileges. But they (picturing the whole human race) brought forth wild grapes – the misery and oppression of a godless society.

The great 'woes' of the Lord are here pronounced against greed, pride, love of power, drunkenness, pleasure-lust, wilful ignorance of divine and profound issues, reversal and perversion of moral values, cheating for personal gain, and other 'liberties' so prized by atheism.

The burden of *Isaiah 5* is to show the unmistakable outcome for all societies characterised by this behaviour. The more prevalent the sin, the greater the bitterness of the consequences.

3. Using personal testimony

Because the atheist is running away from the voice of conscience (the second part of the Lord's analysis of atheism), we must aim at stirring it into life. The use of personal testimony is often effective in achieving this as we see from the provision which Christ made for maintaining a witness to an 'atheistic' community on the eastern shore of Galilee. When the Lord cast out the demons from the possessed man of Gadara, they entered a herd of swine which immediately ran down a steep place to be drowned in the lake. The result was that 'the whole multitude of the country of the Gadarenes round about besought him to depart from them; for they were taken with great fear' *(Luke 8.37)*.

For our purposes, the people of Gadara may fairly be placed in the category of 'atheists', because, while they were Jews, they had spurned and disregarded their religious responsibilities and privileges. (Their heavy involvement with forbidden animals is evidence enough of this.) When they found themselves exposed to a double manifestation of the power of God (a marvellous healing and a judgement), and also to religious instruction, they became desperate for this new influence to leave them. Their consciences were being stirred, and so they wanted the Lord out of their sight and away from their coasts as soon as possible.

This is exactly the spirit of atheism. Should there ever be a pang of conscience, or any spiritual manifestations or evidence, the atheistic heart wants it out of sight and out of mind. It must be smothered with a flurry of rationalistic excuses.

We note that in this case the Lord did not argue with the Gadarene community, but left them with an unanswerable *testimony*. Luke records: 'Now the man out of whom the devils were departed besought him that he might be with him: but Jesus sent him away, saying, Return to thine own house, and shew how great things God hath done unto thee. And he went his way, and published throughout the whole city how great things Jesus had done unto him' *(Luke 8.38-39).*

The method of the Lord was to leave stationed in that region a person with a great personal testimony. There he stood as a living rebuke to unbelief, and as a reminder to all of how God alone can transform character. Our words about our own conversion, and about the spiritual experience of others, will have greater effect than the most sophisticated intellectual reasoning, in the case of atheistic unbelievers.

Let us, then, place the greatest stress on spiritual facts and testimony, rather than an *excess* of indirect reasoning.

4. Exposing the cruelties and impotence of atheism

We are given a strong pointer to the stance we should take with atheists even in the conduct of our Saviour toward Pilate at the time of the crucifixion. Pilate, though shaken within himself, stuck defiantly to his unbelief in the proud and contemptuous words he directed at Christ, saying, 'Speakest thou not unto me? knowest thou not that I have power to crucify thee, and have power to release thee?' *(John 19.10.)*

The Lord had not answered Pilate's previous question, 'Whence art thou?' But now He answered, saying, 'Thou couldest have no power at all against me, except it were given thee from above.'

The lesson is that the atheist is a sinner in the hands of the mighty God, and he must not be encouraged to take the 'superior ground' of a sophisticated, superior thinker, standing in judgement upon the Truth. He must not be allowed to dictate the agenda, and dominate the discussion, conducting it as a lofty inspection of all the perceived weaknesses of Christianity. We must not yield to his line of reasoning, and thereby give him licence to slander God, denigrate the Word, ridicule the work of the Spirit, and pour contempt upon the Lord's people. We should not give him scope to buttress his wicked unbelief with an imagined victory over us.

Our assignment, by the help of the Spirit, is to turn that haughty, inquisitorial judge into a humble, needy seeker after Truth and grace, and we cannot do that by flattering his corrupt intellect, and whimpering under his verbal indignities.

We must try to put the atheist on the run, and attack the gaping holes in his ideas, and the catastrophic results of his moral policies.

We may point to the obvious impotence of atheism to lift up human nature. As in the countries of the old Soviet Union, atheism leads to the stripping of morality, well-being, liberty, dignity, and tenderness from society, opening the way to unimaginable cruelties. In Western society over the last half-century, as belief in God has declined, so the impotence of atheism to reform and improve lives has been manifested.

We must point to the moral cruelties which are so prevalent where there is no fear of God, whether seen in selfishness, violent crime, sexual abuse, child abuse, or in marriage breakdown with all its self-consideration, and callous indifference to children. Atheism equals cruelty, and we should emphasise that. Atheism is behind this selfish society in which everyone looks out for himself.

5. Exposing the intellectual dishonesty of atheism

We should also attack the dishonesty of atheism. Nothing is lower than the way in which atheism campaigns to promote its tenets. Because the 'alternative' society (the anti-moral society) proposed by atheism is so indefensible, it must be presented through fiction, rather than by argument. So the entertainment industry brainwashes the public with a scene of nice, reasonable atheists, and narrow, miserable, hypocritical, bigoted religionists.

Adultery is presented in the soaps as reasonable and inevitable. The very best people are homosexual or lesbian. All may find deep happiness in sensual satisfaction, and so on. Through fiction, the atheistic Utopia is projected to the people, and by ludicrous lies its cause is promoted.

We may also attack the unreasonableness of atheism. To quote Bridges, 'Let them be pressed with their own difficulties – far greater than those of the Gospel.' Why, for example, do evolutionists make no attempt to answer the ever rising tide of dissent from within the scientific world? Why are the many block-buster volumes of recent years *never* responded to? We refer to those tomes from leading men in their fields which appear to utterly refute evolutionary thinking root and branch. Why do the high priests of the evolutionary 'faith' behave in such a grossly unscientific and cowardly manner?

The answer is that these militantly atheistic evolutionists are unreasonable people, who *must* keep the 'faith', because not to do so would sweep away a foundation of atheism. Their evolutionary belief is a faith of the worst kind, maintained in the face of facts which challenge it, and energised solely by prejudice.

We must challenge the atheist about his inability to account for the universe, for life, for the distinction between the human race and the animals, for complexity, for moral consciousness and the faculty of reason, for the instinct of God, for the depravity of man, for the fact of reformation by spiritual conversion, and so on. Atheists have no explanation for any of these things.

6. Emphasising the immortality of the soul

We are given a superb example of how to deal with convinced atheists by the apostle Paul on Mars' Hill *(Acts 17)*. He there encountered Epicurean and Stoic philosophers who, after some discussion, invited him to address the Areopagus, the supreme council of Athens, which regulated the city's religious and educational affairs. Gathered with the elders of Athens (for what was probably an informal session) was a 'public gallery' of interested Athenians and foreigners. Though Paul directed his message to all the outlooks represented, including that of the idolaters, he kept chiefly in mind the Epicureans and Stoics who arranged the meeting. Not that they wanted to learn, but rather to indulge their patronising and scornful curiosity.

These philosophers corresponded very closely to present-day atheists. Epicureans believed that the chief end of life was happiness, and Stoics were rationalists. They did not believe in the immortality of the soul in any *personal*, continuing way.*

Paul's strategy for these philosophers was masterly. He began by speaking against idolatry in a manner which immediately grasped the attention of the Epicureans and the Stoics. To their surprise they found that Paul advanced *some of their own arguments*. They ridiculed idolaters for worshipping gods made by human hands. When they heard Paul saying exactly what they themselves said, their respect was aroused. They had assumed that he would be a teacher of foreign gods – just another idolater.

Paul here used the element of surprise so often employed by our Saviour, and the instant the ears of

---

*The Epicureans (materialists) pursued happiness as the chief purpose of life and believed the soul was merely material. The Stoics (pantheists) regarded the soul as a fragment of the divine principle of the universe which was reabsorbed by the universe at death.

the philosophers were opened, he began to teach them the lofty concept of a spiritual and yet personal God. Next he moved to the subject of personal conversion, and the fact of a coming day of judgement, no doubt including the atonement as he spoke of the resurrection.

Today many atheists sneer at the Christian faith because they see absurd distortions. They deride a religion which has its representative clergymen on both sides of a war, all blessing the troops in the name of God. They remember the clergy who visited the schools in their childhood, and the effete nonsense they spoke. They observe the insincerity and confusion so evident in much of the apostate Anglican church.

Sometimes, it does not hurt to agree with the atheist, and so surprise him, opening his mind to our point of view. We can agree with his condemnation of 'state' religion, or any other formal and spiritually lifeless variety of religion. In doing this we dissociate ourselves from error and clear away some of the misconceptions cluttering the mind of the atheist. We aim to show, as the apostle showed his hearers, that the true religion is altogether different. It has nothing in common with the naive and foolish caricature in the atheist's mind.

In *1 Corinthians 15.32* Paul condemns the motto of atheism, 'Let us eat and drink; for to morrow we die.' 'What point is there,' they say, 'in worrying about God or morals, if there is no afterlife? Let us do what we like, for when death comes, that will be the end!'

In seeking to stir the concern of atheists we remember what the older writers said about their viewpoint. They liked to point out that atheists are great gamblers. Their entire outlook, lifestyle and policy depends on the assumption that death is the end. But what if they are wrong? In all witness we must persistently chip away at this assumption, for it is their weakest and most vulnerable point.

We must speak of eternity, of the coming day, and of the reality of Heaven and hell. For many an atheist this will be the challenge causing greatest unease.

Everything in the world, to atheists, is material and nothing but material. All has come about by sheer chance. There is no Designer, no Creator, no ultimate purpose and no eternity. Our most effective and *dis*-comforting testimony, will be to speak often of our eternal hope, and to stress the reality of our experience of God's power and blessing.

In his ministry to atheistic philosophers Paul emphasised the *authority* and *sovereignty* of God, Who has fixed the life span of every human soul. He stressed the *personal* character of God, Who must be sought by men and women in order to be *found* and *known*. He spoke of the need for repentance, of the coming day of judgement, and of the resurrection and afterlife. These are the themes of our witness to atheists.

9. Prepared for Questions

ANSWERING QUESTIONS is the stuff of personal witness, and the believer must be well prepared. If we do not know how to respond to typical questions we will stumble at the finest opportunities. Indeed, some of the chief biblical exhortations to witness warn that we must be ready for questions. Peter tells us to 'be ready always to give an answer to every man that asketh you a reason of the hope that is in you.' Paul says: 'Let your speech be alway with grace . . . that ye may know how ye ought to answer every man.'

God forbid that we should be forced to deal with questions as the politicians do. When asked a question, the politician ignores it and answers a different question. The result is mistrust, boredom and contempt.

Why should people want to hear the answer to a question they never asked?

The Lord's way of dealing with questions is the perfect model for us. He did not necessarily give the kind of answer which His questioners expected, but neither did He duck or avoid the question. He always gave the *spiritual* answer, and thus provided light on the way of salvation. People asked Him many questions, some of these being only in their minds or murmured amongst themselves, but He knew their thoughts, and answered them. The Jewish leaders also asked questions, usually to trap Him and make Him appear heretical or foolish.

We, too, hear many hostile and defensive questions, and we must learn how to turn them to account so that we may minister to the souls of our questioners.

First, some general observations on questions will be profitable. We observe that the Lord never answered at great length, and neither should we. Too much talking is the ruin of witness. The writer remembers the excitement of a lady who went out visiting homes in her neighbourhood, knocking on doors and telling people about the Lord. In a single week she gained admission into two flats in the same block, and spent a couple of hours in each presenting the Gospel, and answering questions at great length. The following week, to her distress, no one in that entire block would answer their door, although she knew the people were in.

A long answer to a question outstays our welcome, and future witness is imperilled. Like the Lord, we must be self-disciplined and fairly brief. (Remember also that the Lord's longest answers were in the interesting form of parables or illustrations.)

But what is a 'spiritual' answer to a question? It is an answer which provides a *spiritual* explanation for the problem. Take, for example, the question asked by the Jews in the Nazareth synagogue at the time that the Lord began His ministry. They wondered at His 'gracious words', but they were perplexed and offended that a carpenter should teach in such a way, and they said, 'Is not this Joseph's son?'

The simple answer would have been, 'Yes.' A longer answer might have explained that He was not strictly Joseph's son, but certainly Mary's, and proceeded to explain why their Messiah had entered the world through a humble family. The *spiritual* answer in this case was to show why the question had been asked, and to expose the prejudice which lay behind it. 'I tell you of a truth,' said the Lord, 'many widows were in Israel in the days of Elias . . . when great famine was throughout all the land; but unto none of them was Elias sent, save unto Sarepta, a city of Sidon, unto a woman that was a widow.'

Similarly, He told them how only Naaman the Syrian was healed, and not any of the Jewish lepers in Israel in the days of Elisha. Prejudice and unbelief among the Jews had cut off the blessing of God before, and it had gone to gentiles. The Lord laid His finger on their unbelief, and challenged their hearts.

When the scribes and Pharisees criticised the conduct of the Lord's disciples, saying, 'Why do ye eat and drink with publicans and sinners?' Christ answered in terms of His spiritual mission. 'I came not to call the righteous, but sinners to repentance.' At another time, when they demanded to know precisely when the kingdom of God would come, He replied in terms of the *spiritual* kingdom of God ruling in hearts, saying, 'The kingdom of God cometh not with observation . . . for, behold, the kingdom of God is within you.' The implication was that not all Jews were members of this kingdom, but only those who had God truly in their hearts.

The chief priest and the scribes, seeking to accuse Him of treason, slyly asked, 'Is it lawful for us to give tribute unto Caesar, or no?' And He replied by showing the difference between earthly duties and heavenly duties. In the case of the woman taken in adultery the rulers said, 'Moses in the law commanded us, that such should be stoned: but what sayest thou?' And the Lord answered in such a manner that their own consciences were stirred, and their sin condemned.

Questions, therefore, are the most wonderful opportunities to give spiritual explanations. Even though the purpose of the questioner may be to confuse the issue, create a diversion, or even to scoff, we may be able to make a spiritual response and application. To train for this it is a good idea to write down all the questions which are heard repeatedly, and set ourselves the task of writing up good answers for future use. Where churches organise regular neighbourhood visitation, it is helpful for younger believers to be teamed up with experienced visitors so that they may learn how they deal with the questions.

A number of key questions, with answers, have been assembled by the author in evangelistic 'magazines', and these may prove helpful, not only as hand-out literature, but for suggesting answers to those engaged in witness.* The answers provided are derived from ten-minute talks broadcast some years ago. Here are some of the questions:–

Why does God allow wars, sickness and tragedies? The answer, among other things, explains human rebellion, and speaks of how the human race has fouled up its world, cut itself off from God, become God's bitter enemy, and forfeited His help.

How can I be sure there is a God? The answer ranges briefly across the evidence of design and complexity, together with the strange condition of human beings, possessing the power of reason and moral conscience, coupled with hopeless weakness and tendency to

---

*Details are provided on the end-pages of this book.

failure. It is shown that only the biblical explanation accounts for such things. The answer also points out that the ultimate proof of God is available only to those who seek and find Him.

The offensive type of question is also included, such as – *How can we be expected to take Christianity seriously? It is so narrow. You have to be so naive about life.* Here is a kind of protest question which needs to be courteously but firmly turned round to show that the non-Christian is the narrow and naive person, cut off from divine resources.

Why are there so many religions? To be asked such a question is a gift to the regular witnesser, who will point to the instinct for God which leads people to be religious, and also expose their motives in inventing religions of their own, rather than accepting the true faith. It is an opportunity to explain why a *revealed* religion is so essential, and that only such a message could be authentic.

How can a God of love send people to hell? The answer is all Gospel, as the holiness and justice of God are explained, together with the necessity of forgiveness and new life. Human unbelief and rebellion is shown to be a vote against God and Heaven, which will be 'honoured' by God in the last day.

Is not religion just for the inadequate and dependent personality? This is a question representative of the proud and contemptuous type, and it is best answered by a portrayal of non-believing people as those who are *determined* to be restricted and limited in their lives. They opt for an incomplete existence, lacking spiritual knowledge and power, and living at the mercy of the material world.

These evangelistic magazines include short articles on archaeological evidence which supports the accuracy of the biblical record, and also on the fallacy of evolution. These provide an example of how such themes may be presented to challenge the brainwashed secular mind, but not at great length, as though our witness depended on providing rational proof for the existence of God. Apologetic material, we contend, is useful and interesting to the unbeliever, but a hindrance if pursued excessively.

These brief comments on the importance and usefulness of questions can barely touch the surface of the subject. An entire manual of suggested answers to different questions could usefully be compiled to help the ministry of personal witness.[*]

In answering questions our aim is to present the Lord, rather than to become entangled with the details

---

[*]There are excellent books available to answer questions from people becoming involved in cults, such as the Jehovah's Witnesses and the Mormons – *JWs Answered Verse by Verse,* by David A. Reed, *Mormons Answered Verse by Verse,* by David A. Reed & John R. Farkas (both published by Baker Book House, USA, and Wakeman Trust, UK).

of each question. It is important to remember that with the spiritual ignorance of the present day, people are often surprised to have very obvious matters explained. To emphasise in our answers that God is a *personal* God, and an approachable God, not an impersonal force, is most helpful to people. This is what their instincts tell them, but in an age when pantheistic ideas are all-pervasive, it is reassuring to have this stressed.

The *manner* in which questions are answered requires close personal monitoring. Some witnessing believers are inclined to get carried away, and to come across badly to their hearers. The text with which we began this chapter must be taken seriously. Peter says, 'But sanctify the Lord God in your hearts: and be ready always to give an answer to every man that asketh you a reason of the hope that is in you *with meekness and fear.*'

This is a spiritual work. We are not defending our own opinions, but representing Almighty God. Our object is not to appear knowledgeable, or to win arguments, but to represent sincerely a perfect God and a saving message. Questions must be answered humbly, reverently, helpfully and courteously. They must be answered in full awareness of the possibility that God the Holy Spirit could well use our answers in the course of His regenerating, converting work in a soul.

Certainly we would not want the smallest trace of

arrogance, haughtiness, over-confidence, impatience or peevishness to taint or ruin our answers in the estimation of our questioner, and our prayers and efforts will be directed to ensure that this shall never be so.

We conclude this glance at the need to prepare for questions with a comment on the way to send souls to Christ the Saviour. The chief end of all witness, including the answering of questions, is to urge lost people to go to Christ in prayer, and to seek His salvation. It is true that not every opportunity for witness, or every question answered, affords an appropriate moment for us to give our hearer a personal exhortation to seek the Lord. Naturally, we must be wise about this. On some occasions, it may be more appropriate to express the need to seek the Lord in a general rather than personal way. We may, for instance, say, 'Those who seek the Lord will be blessed,' rather than, '*You* must seek the Lord, or *you* will be eternally lost.'

Some readers may have picked up Arminian phraseology, so that they find themselves wanting to say, 'You must receive Christ into your life.' This kind of expression is not only likely to confuse people, but it makes witness more difficult. It is much more natural, more understandable, and, of course, more biblical to bring the witness to conclusion with an exhortation along these lines – 'If you sincerely ask the Saviour for forgiveness and new life, you will receive it.' The biblical rule is that needy souls must be directed to apply to Him; to go to Him.

The Lord Himself said, 'Come unto Me!' He did not say to sinners, 'Ask Me to come to you. Ask Me into your lives.' Never forget the direction of the Lord's own exhortation to salvation in *Luke 11.9-10*. It is Godward! 'And I say unto you, Ask, and it shall be given you; seek, and ye shall find; knock, and it shall be opened unto you. For every one that asketh receiveth; and he that seeketh findeth; and to him that knocketh it shall be opened.' The direction is important. We send people to Him, and as we do so we pray for them, that God will overrule in their hearts, and that they will trust Him, and go to Him.

The Lord has ordained the ministry of personal witness, and He will not let us go on in the work unblessed. In the giving of the great commission, our ever faithful Lord said, 'Lo, I am with you alway, even unto the end of the world.' He gave His people also the great promise of fruitfulness, saying, 'Ye have not chosen me, but I have chosen you, and ordained you, that ye should go and bring forth fruit, and that your fruit should remain' *(John 15.16)*. The Lord will certainly bless His loyal servants, and strengthen and encourage, until the day they hear His matchless voice saying, 'Well done, thou good and faithful servant: thou hast been faithful over a few things . . . enter thou into the joy of thy lord' *(Matthew 25.21)*.

Evangelistic Publications
by Dr Peter Masters
(all available through the Wakeman Trust)

Magazine format evangelistic booklets:

Answers to Questions 1 & 2

These well-known 'magazines' have been repeatedly reprinted in enormous quantities over the years. They are admirably suited for neighbourhood distribution, or for use in conjunction with personal witness. Many churches have employed them for mass-distribution. Experience shows that they are read with interest, and tend to be taken more seriously than leaflet-format tracts. Each is 12 pages, 9½" x 7½".

Answers to Questions 1

Includes articles answering – How can I be sure there is a God? Why does God allow wars, sickness and tragedies? Were we designed or did we evolve? Isn't the Christian message narrow?

Answers to Questions 2

Includes articles answering – Why are there so many different religions? What exactly is conversion? How could a God of love send people to hell? How can we accept the myths of the Bible?

Unseen World

Includes articles entitled – Time the Mysterious Dimension; Is Death a Conscious Experience? Waveband of the Soul (how to pray); Check Your Health! (a spiritual health check).

A5-size evangelistic booklets:

The Cruelties of Atheism

This booklet exposes the motive for atheism (the desire to get rid of moral restraints), and then shows its unreasonableness, its dishonest methods, its militant 'agenda', its failure to improve people's lives, and its immensely cruel results. Here is a view of atheism as God sees it, together with a way to escape its effects, through salvation.

The Rebellious Years

Subtitled *The Need for Self-Understanding*, this is intended to help readers from mid-teenage to late twenties to understand the source of the inner rebellion that presses them away from God in the 'second quarter' of life. Most people during these years experience strong urges for independence, sometimes with deep suspicion of everything around them, and a strong inclination to disbelieve in God. Here is help for the young to recognise the process behind their moral reaction, and to believe the Gospel.

How to Seek and Find the Lord

Intended for seekers or those more open to help, the author emphasises that there is only one way of salvation, clearly defined and revealed by God in His Word. He then explains the kind of belief and attitude which brings a seeker to find the Lord.

A booklet for those who witness:

Seven Certain Signs of True Conversion

Dr Masters here lists the biblical indications that a person has been truly converted, so that those who witness for

Christ and help seekers may know how to give correct counsel and advice. Examples of right and wrong counsel are provided.

Books to help in evangelism:

Men of Destiny and *Men of Purpose* are two very popular volumes of Christian biography, presenting the lives and conversion experiences of 25 famous, unusual or even notorious people, including royals, Reformers, and 'fathers' of modern science.

Given to unconverted people, these books challenge the heart and open the way to further spiritual influence. For the preacher, youth leader or Sunday School teacher, they provide outstanding testimonies to illustrate and enrich messages for years to come.

Men of Destiny
172 pages, paperback, illustrated, ISBN 1 870855 03 5

Tsar Alexander Pavlovich *(The tsar who defeated Napoleon)*
Lieut 'Birdie' Bowers *(Scott's 'bravest man' in the Antarctic)*
Sir James Simpson *(The discoverer of anaesthetic chloroform)*
Alves Reis *(The counterfeiter who nearly owned his country)*
Joshua Poole *(The story of 'Fiddler Joss', drunkard turned preacher)*
Viscount Alexander of Hillsborough *(A leader of the House of Lords)*
John Newton *(The transformed slave-trader)*
Jean Henri Dunant *(Founder of the International Red Cross)*
Martin Luther *(The ex-monk who led the Reformation)*
Bilney, Tyndale & Latimer *(Three heroic English martyrs)*
Alfred the Great *(The king who organised England)*
Lieut-General Sir William Dobbie *(World War II hero of Malta)*

Men of Purpose
167 pages, paperback, illustrated, ISBN 1 870855 04 3

Michael Faraday *(Father of electrical science)*
Henry J. Heinz *(Founder of the food empire)*
Felix Mendelssohn *(A composer with a spiritual journey)*
Lord Radstock *(Whose missions brought conversions to Russia's aristocracy)*
James Clerk Maxwell *(Father of modern physics)*
Philip P. Bliss *(The hymnwriter who won countless souls)*
Fred Charrington *(The brewer who renounced a fortune)*
Lord Kelvin *(Britain's greatest scientific inventor)*
James Montgomery *(A poet who ran away from God)*
Sir John Ambrose Fleming *(Inventor of the radio valve)*
Daniel Defoe *(The founder of journalism and great novelist)*

The Necessity of Sunday Schools
In this Post-Christian Era
Peter Masters & Malcolm H. Watts
112 pages, paperback, ISBN 1 870855 13 2

A clarion call for the unique effectiveness of *evangelistic* Sunday Schools operated on a large scale. This book offers invincible proof that the Bible sanctions and commands child evangelism of the kind represented by vigorous Sunday School outreach. The authors contend that there is no need for Sunday School numbers to fall, or for Schools to close. Christians should take a 'total neighbourhood responsibility' for the rising generation. Here is real stimulation and encouragement for the opening or enlargement of Sunday Schools, along with counsel and help for workers.

Other Wakeman titles by Dr Masters:

Only One Baptism of the Holy Spirit
109 pages, paperback, ISBN 1 870855 17 5

The Healing Epidemic
227 pages, paperback, ISBN 1 870855 00 0

The Charismatic Phenomenon
(Peter Masters & John C. Whitcomb)
113 pages, paperback, ISBN 1 870855 01 9

Should Christians Drink?
112 pages, paperback, ISBN 1 870855 12 4

The Baptist Confession of Faith of 1689
(updated with notes by Dr Peter Masters)
91 pages, paperback, ISBN 1 870855 02 7

*World Dominion – The High Ambition of
Reconstructionism*
52 pages, paperback, ISBN 1 870855 16 7

These books are available from Christian bookshops, or
from the publisher: The Wakeman Trust, 5 Templar Street,
London SE5 9JB. Tel: 071-735 7989